WORLD HISTORY ATLAS

A collection of maps illustrating geographically the most significant periods and events in the history of civilization.

EUROPE
PHYSICAL

Copyright by C. S. HAMMOND & Co., N. Y.

TABLE OF CONTENTS

	Page No.
The Cradles of Civilization, 3000-1000 B. C.	H-2
Major States and Empires in 500 B. C.	H-2
Major States and Empires in 400 A. D.	H-2
The Expansion of Western Civilization, 1600 A. D.	H-2
The Assyrian Empire, 824 to 625 B. C.	H-3
Great Empires of the Sixth Century B. C.	H-3
The Biblical World	H-4
Ancient Greece (Hellas)	H-4
a. Ancient Athens	
b. Crete	
The Persian Empire and the Empire of Alexander the Great	H-5
The Roman Empire about 117 A. D.	H-5
Ancient Italy before Augustus	H-6
a. The Forum, Capitolium and Palatium	
b. Imperial Fora	
c. Environs of Rome	
d. Rome under the Emperors	
e. Rome in the Time of the Republic	
Europe showing Barbaric Migrations in the IV and V Centuries	H-7
Europe 600 A. D.	H-8
Europe c. 800 A. D.	H-9
a. Treaty of Verdun, 843	
b. Treaty of Mersen, 870	
c. Final Partition, 888	
Britannia about 350 A. D.	H-10
English Conquest from 450 to End of the VI Century	H-10
England in the VIII Century (The "Heptarchy")	H-10
England after the Peace of Wedmore (878 A. D.)	H-10
The Expansion of Islam, 622-700 A. D.	H-11
The Expansion of Islam, 700-900 A. D.	H-11
Europe and the Byzantine Empire about 1000 A. D.	H-12
Mediterranean Lands in 1097	H-13
a. The Califate in 750	
Mediterranean Lands after 1204	H-13
a. Latin States in Syria	
Historical Map of Asia	H-14
Europe c. 1200 A. D.	H-15
Ecclesiastical Map of Europe c. 1300 A. D.	H-16
Economic Map of Europe in the Middle Ages, 1300 A. D.	H-17
English Possessions in France, 1066 to 1272	H-18
France at the Death of Philip IV (The Fair), 1314	H-18
France at the Peace of Bretigny, 1360	H-18
France at the Death of Henry V, 1422	H-18
The Principal Voyages of Discovery to America, 1492-1611	H-19
Europe in 1559	H-20
Europe in 1648 at the Peace of Westphalia	H-21
Europe in 1713-1714 at the Treaties of Utrecht and Rastatt	H-22
Changing Ownership of the Continent	H-22
a. 1682	
b. 1713	
c. 1763	
d. 1783	
French and Indian War, 1756 to 1763	H-22
a. The Principal Battleground in the French and Indian War	

	Page No.
Europe in 1763	H-23
Poland to 1667	H-24
Poland — Result of the 1st Partition, 1772	H-24
Poland — Result of the 2nd Partition, 1793	H-24
Poland — Result of the 3rd Partition, 1795	H-24
France at the Outbreak of the Revolution — Inequalities of the Salt Tax	H-25
Paris at the Outbreak of the Revolution	H-25
Western Germany at the Outbreak of the French Revolution	H-26
Europe in 1803	H-26
Europe in 1812 at the Height of Napoleon's Power	H-27
Europe after the Congress of Vienna, 1815 to 1839	H-28
The Colonization of Latin America	H-29
Latin American Countries since the Colonial Period	H-29
Italy at the Close of the XV Century	H-30
Unification of Italy, 1859 to 1924	H-30
Central Europe, 1815 to 1871	H-31
Language Map of Europe, 1910	H-31
England before the Industrial Revolution, c. 1701	H-32
England after the Industrial Revolution	H-32
The Growth of the Ottoman Empire, 1299-1672	H-33
The Decline of the Ottoman Empire, 1699-1923	H-33
The Growth of Russia, covering the period from 1054 to 1914	H-34
Africa in 1914	H-35
Asia in 1914	H-35
Europe in 1914	H-36
The First World War, 1914-1918	H-37
a. Europe and the Near East	
b. The Western Front	
Europe, 1919 to 1929	H-38
The World, 1919 to 1938, Major Powers and Nations with Overseas Territories	H-39
Europe, 1930 to 1939	H-40
The Far East, 1930 to 1941	H-40
The World at War, 1939 to 1945	H-41
European Theatre of War, 1939 to 1945	H-42
Far Eastern Theatre of War, 1941 to 1945	H-42
Europe in 1941	H-43
Present Day Europe	H-44
The Retreat of Colonialism in the Post-War Period	H-45
The World of the United Nations and the Cold War	H-46
Europe — Physical	H-47
World — Population Distribution	H-48

Published by

HAMMOND
INCORPORATED

MAPLEWOOD, NEW JERSEY

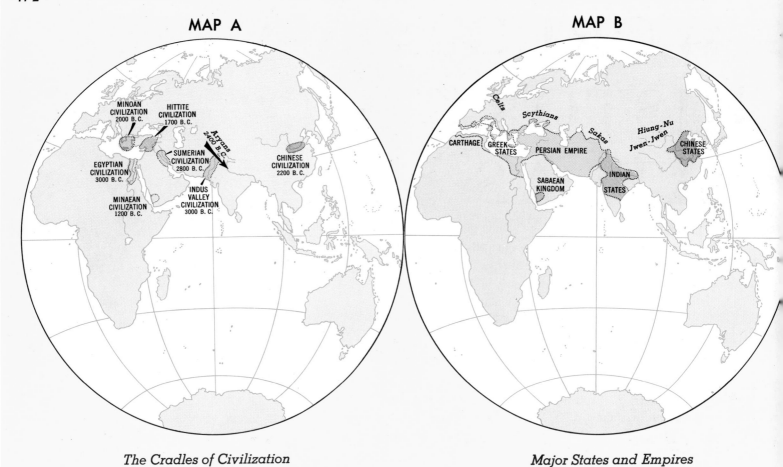

MAP A

The Cradles of Civilization
3000-1000 B.C.

MAP B

Major States and Empires
in 500 B.C.

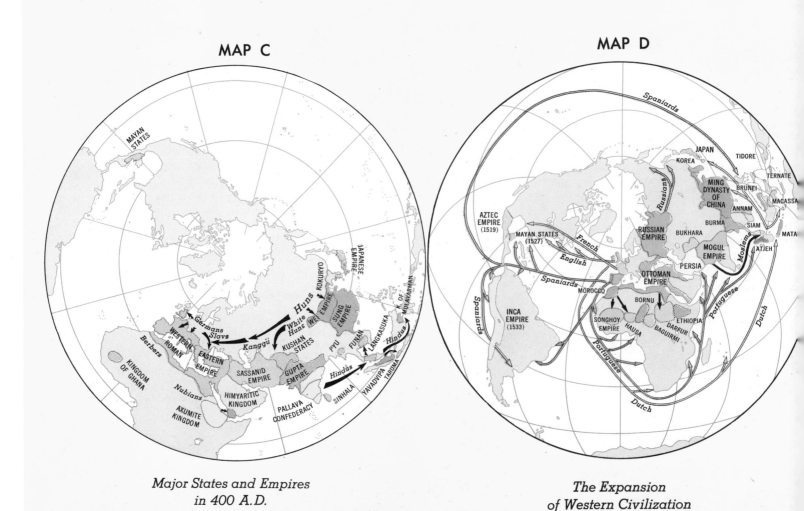

MAP C

Major States and Empires
in 400 A.D.

MAP D

The Expansion
of Western Civilization
1600 A.D.

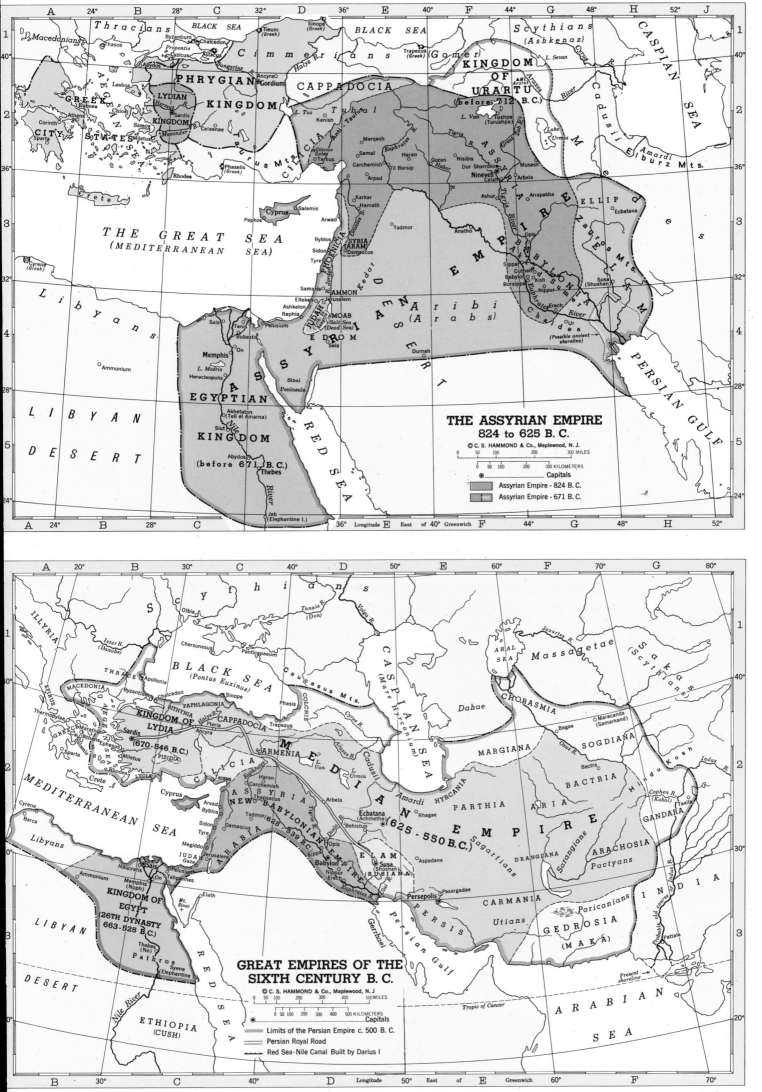

THE ASSYRIAN EMPIRE
824 to 625 B.C.

© C. S. HAMMOND & Co., Maplewood, N.J.

| 0 | 50 | 100 | 200 | 300 MILES |

| 0 | 50 100 | 200 | 300 KILOMETERS |

⊙---------- Capitals

Assyrian Empire - 824 B.C.

Assyrian Empire - 671 B.C.

GREAT EMPIRES OF THE
SIXTH CENTURY B.C.

© C. S. HAMMOND & Co., Maplewood, N.J.

| 0 | 50 | 100 | 200 | 300 | 400 | 500 MILES |

| 0 | 50 100 | 200 | 300 | 400 | 500 KILOMETERS |

⊙ Capitals

Limits of the Persian Empire c. 500 B.C.

Persian Royal Road

Red Sea - Nile Canal Built by Darius I

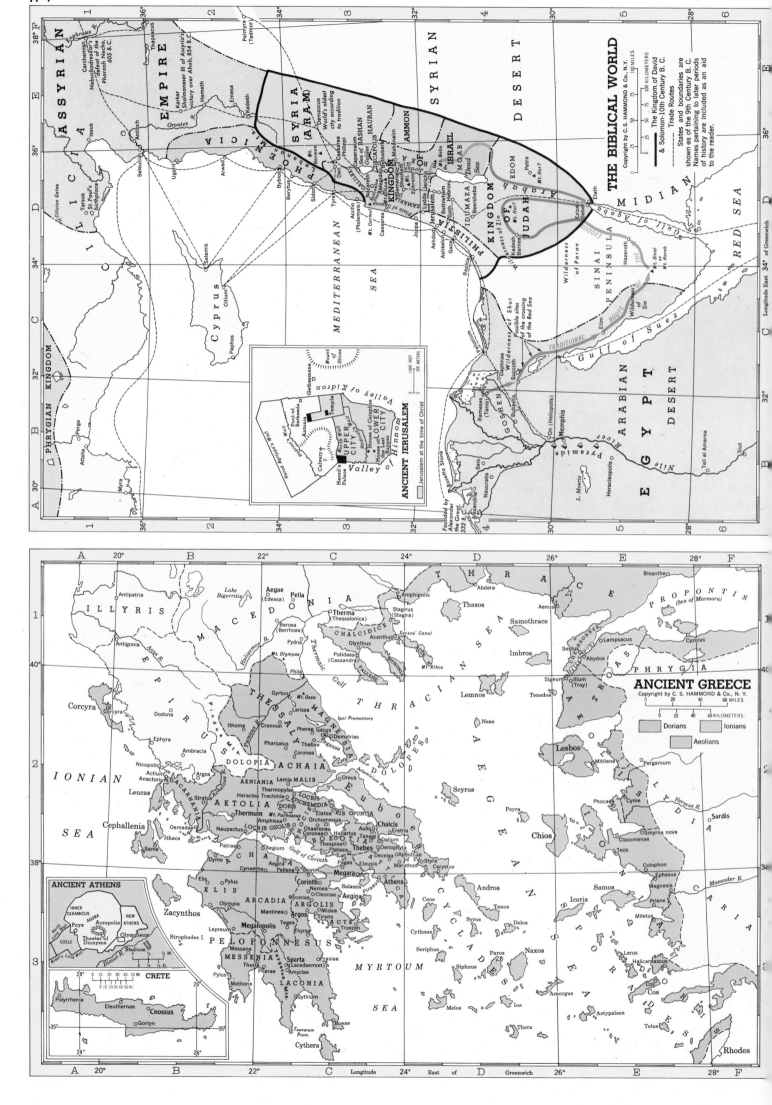

THE BIBLICAL WORLD

Copyright by C. S. HAMMOND & Co., N.Y.

— The Kingdom of David & Solomon-10th Century B.C.

— Trade Routes

States and boundaries are shown as of the 9th Century B.C. Names pertaining to later periods of history are included as an aid to the reader.

0 25 50 75 100 KILOMETERS
0   25   50   75   100 MILES

ANCIENT JERUSALEM
Jerusalem at the time of Christ

ANCIENT GREECE
Copyright by C. S. HAMMOND & Co., N.Y.

0   20   40   60 MILES
0   20   40   60 KILOMETERS

Dorians

Ionians

Aeolians

ANCIENT ATHENS

CRETE

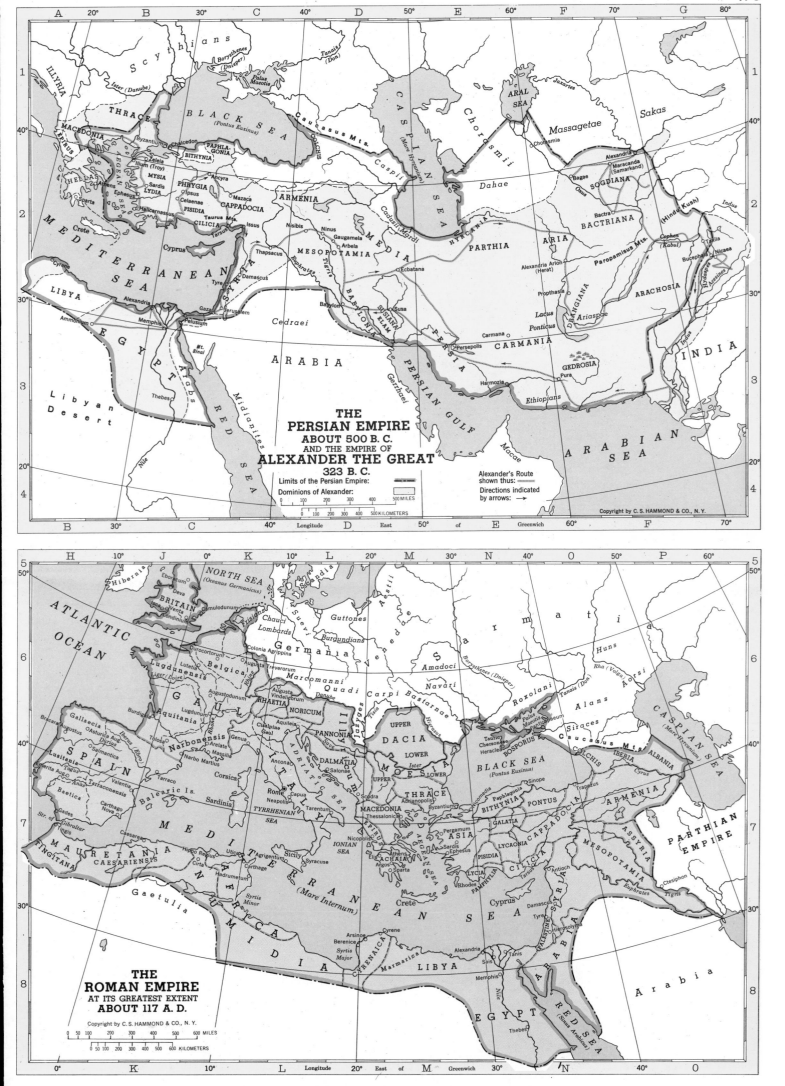

ANCIENT ITALY
ITALIA, LIGURIA, VENETIA, GALLIA-CISALPINA, HISTRIA, SICILIA & CORSICA
Before the time of Augustus

Copyright by C.S. HAMMOND & CO., N.Y.

Roman Colonies, thus: --------- **Ostia**
Greek Colonies, thus: **SYRACUSAE (G)**
Carthaginian Colonies, thus: ----- Eryx (C)
Dotted lines show the Modern shore line

THE FORUM CAPITOLIUM and PALATIUM
1. Templum Saturni
2. Templum Concordiae
3. Scalae Gemoniae
4. Carcer (Tullianum)
5. Senaculum
6. Graecostasis
7. Rostra
8. Templum Jani

IMPERIAL FORA
1. Scalae Gemoniae
2. Templum Vespasiani
3. Porticus Deorum Consentium
4. Equus Caesaris
5. T. Castoris et Pollucis
6. Templum Divi Julii
7. Arcus Augusti
8. Arcus Titi
9. Templum Antonini et Faustinae

ROME
Under the Emperors
1. Templum Jovis Capitolini
2. Arx
3. Forum Romanum
4. Templum Aesculapii
5. Forum Trajani
6. Forum Augusti
7. Porta Carmentalis
8. Arcus Septimii Severi
9. Arcus Constantini
10. Arcus Titi
11. Arcus Claudii
12. Arcus Tiberii
13. Arcus Gallieni
14. Arcus Marci Aurelii
15. Arcus Diocletiani
16. Porta Flumentara
17. Templum Mercurii
18. Theatrum Marcelli

REGIONES AUGUSTI
I. Porta Capena
II. Caelimontium
III. Isis et Serapis
IV. Templum Pacis
V. Esquiliae
VI. Alta Semita
VII. Via Lata
VIII. Forum Romanum
IX. Circus Flaminius
X. Palatium
XI. Circus Maximus
XII. Piscina Publica
XIII. Aventinus
XIV. Trans Tiberim

ROME
In the time of the Republic

EUROPE
SHOWING BARBARIC MIGRATIONS
IN THE
FOURTH AND FIFTH CENTURIES

Copyright by C.S. HAMMOND & CO., N.Y.

Legend:
- Goths
- Huns
- Alans, Suevi, Vandals
- Angles, Saxons, Jutes
- Western Roman Empire
- Eastern Roman Empire

Scale: 100 200 300 400 500 MILES
100 200 300 400 500 KILOMETERS

NORTH SEA

ATLANTIC OCEAN

BALTIC SEA

BLACK SEA

ADRIATIC SEA

MEDITERRANEAN SEA

BRITANNIA / BRITAIN

SPAIN

ITALY

AFRICA PROCONSULATE

NUMIDIA

MAURETANIA

TRIPOLITANIA

EGYPT

SYRIA

MESOPOTAMIA

ARMENIA

CAPPADOCIA

GALATIA

PONTUS

BITHYNIA

PHRYGIA

LYDIA

CARIA

LYCAONIA

PISIDIA

PAMPHYLIA

CILICIA

MYSIA

THRACE

MOESIA (LOWER)

MOESIA (UPPER)

DACIA

MACEDONIA

EPIRUS

PANNONIA

ILLYRICUM

NORICUM

RHAETIA

DALMATIA

GAUL

AQUITANIA

TARRACONENSIS

CARTHAGINENSIS

LUSITANIA

GALLAECIA

Hadrian's Wall

Constantinople

Rome

Carthage

Ravenna

Mediolanum (Milan)

Aquileia

Lugdunum (Lyons)

Lutetia

Colonia

Treveri (Trier)

Genua (Genoa)

Alexandria

Antioch

Damascus

Jerusalem (Hierosolyma)

Cyprus

Crete

Rhodes

Corsica

Sardinia

Sicily

Balearic Is.

Str. of Gibraltar (Tangier)

West Goths, East Goths, Visigoths (Thervingi), Ostrogoths (Greutungi)

Vandals, Alans, Suevi

Huns, Attila, Attila's Capital?

Burgundians, Lombards, Rugians, Scirians, Heruli, Gepids

Quadi, Jazyges, Marcomanni, Basternae

Wends (Northern Slavs), Antes (Southern Slavs), Esthonians

Franks, Salian Franks, Ripuarian Franks, Alamanni

Saxons, Angles, Jutes, Frisians, Thuringians

Picts, Scots, Britons

Alaric, Athaulf, Gaiseric

Pollentia (Alaric 402), Alaric died 410

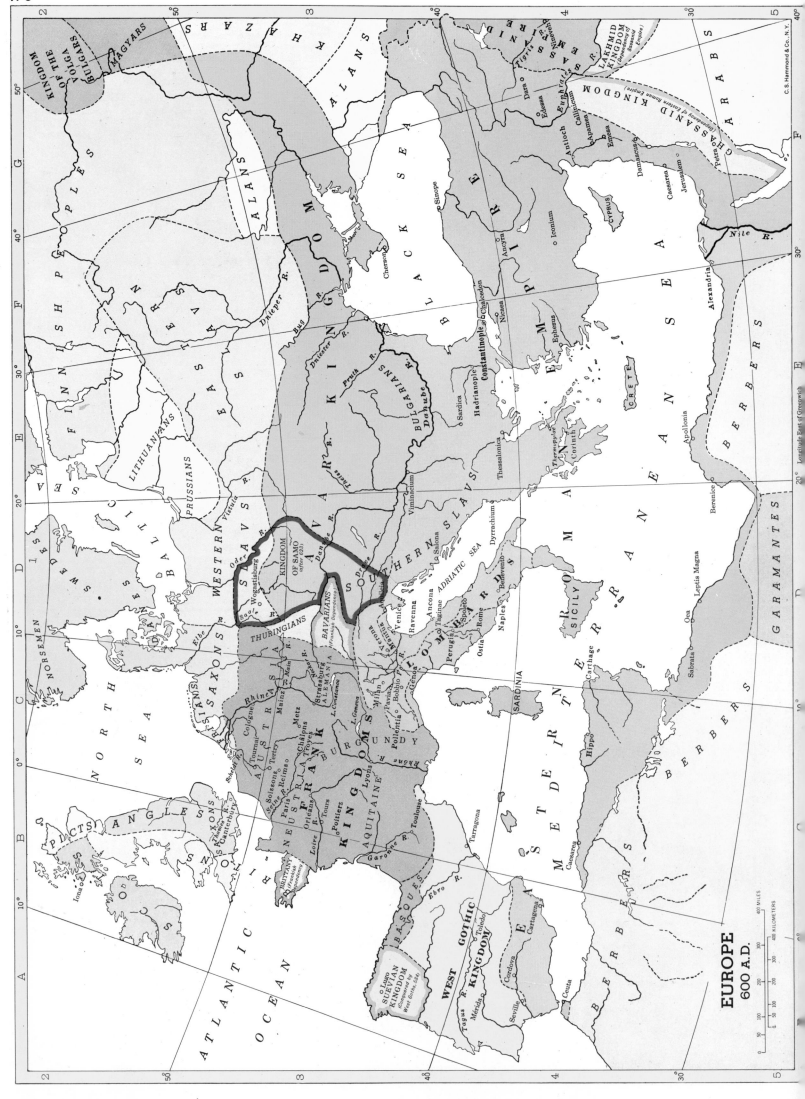

EUROPE
600 A.D.

C. S. Hammond & Co., N.Y.

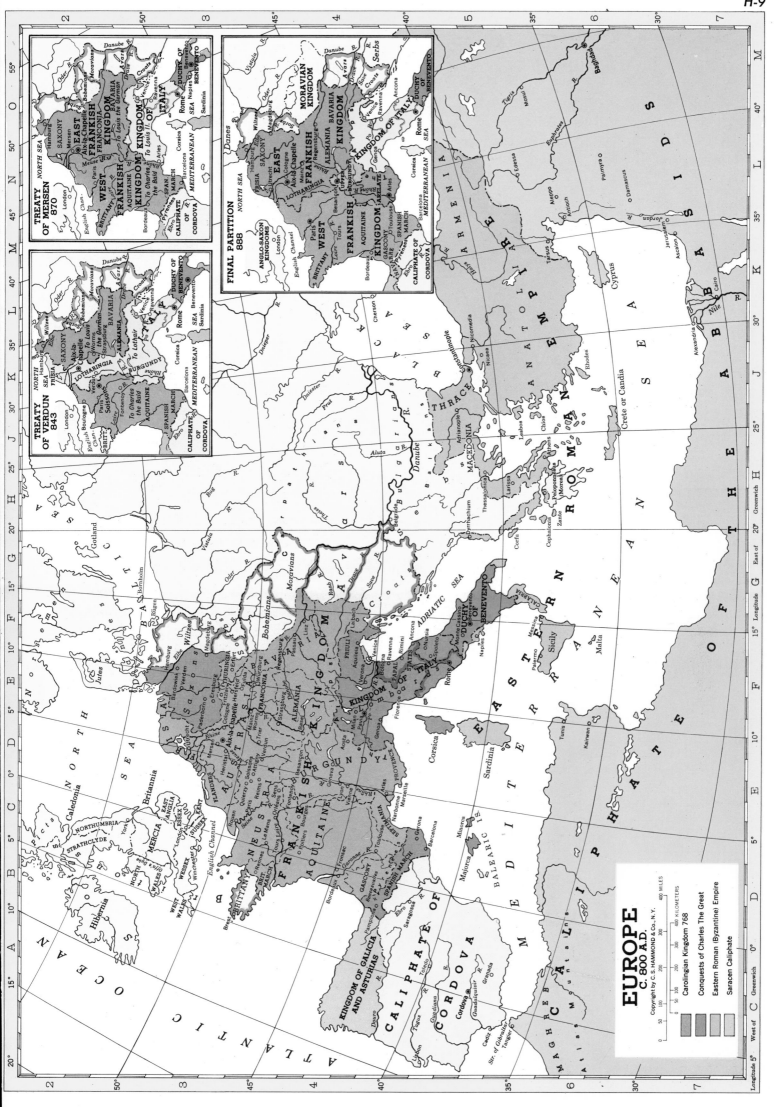

EUROPE
C. 800 A.D.

Copyright by C. S. HAMMOND & CO., N.Y.

- Carolingian Kingdom 768
- Conquests of Charles The Great
- Eastern Roman (Byzantine) Empire
- Saracen Caliphate

TREATY OF VERDUN 843

TREATY OF MERSEN 870

FINAL PARTITION 888

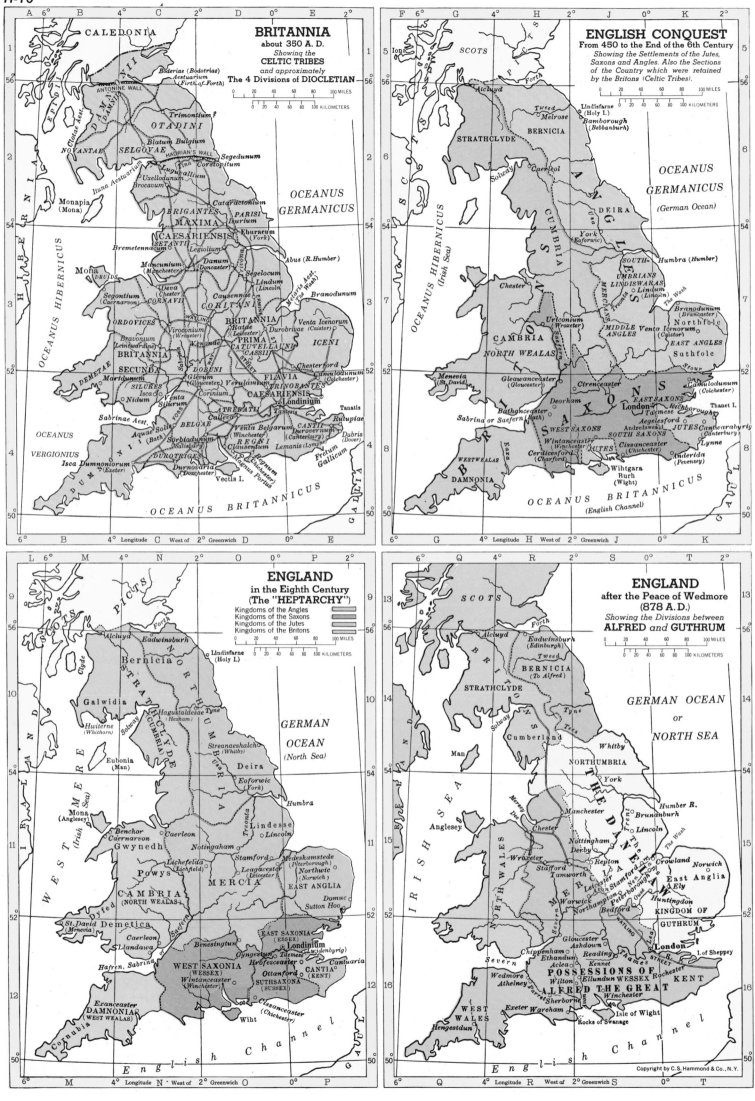

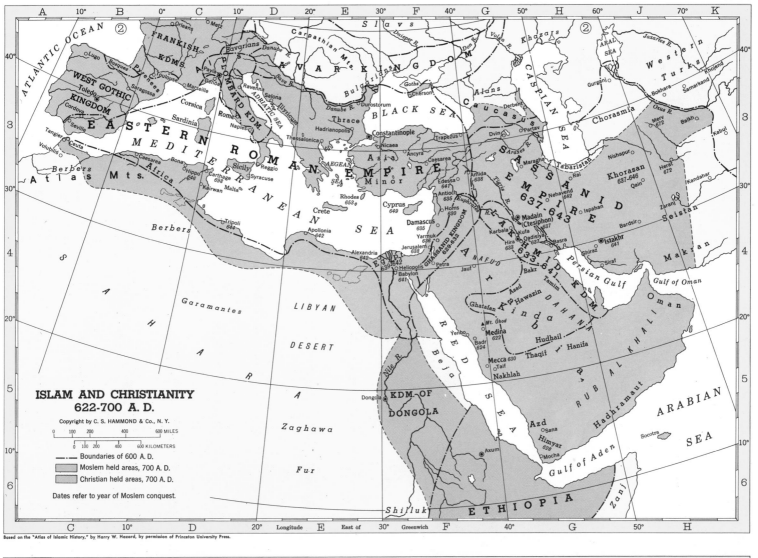

ISLAM AND CHRISTIANITY
622-700 A.D.

Copyright by C. S. HAMMOND & Co., N.Y.

Boundaries of 600 A.D.
Moslem held areas, 700 A.D.
Christian held areas, 700 A.D.

Dates refer to year of Moslem conquest.

Based on the "Atlas of Islamic History," by Harry W. Hazard, by permission of Princeton University Press.

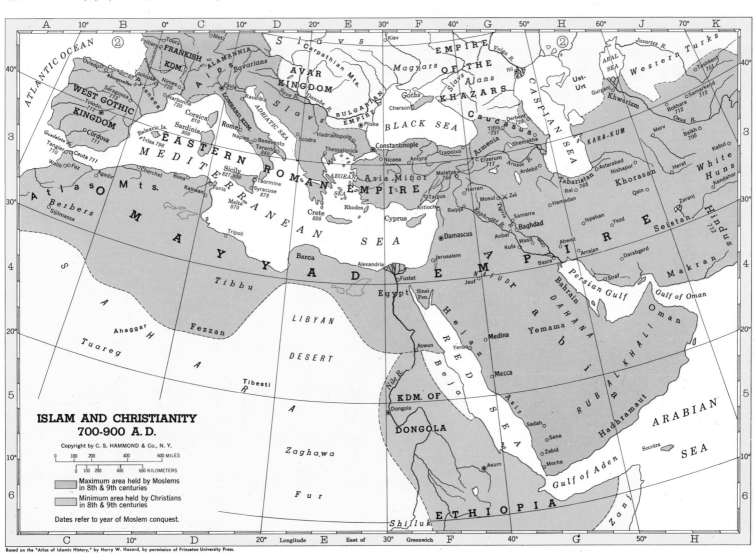

ISLAM AND CHRISTIANITY
700-900 A.D.

Copyright by C. S. HAMMOND & Co., N.Y.

Maximum area held by Moslems in 8th & 9th centuries
Minimum area held by Christians in 8th & 9th centuries

Dates refer to year of Moslem conquest.

Based on the "Atlas of Islamic History," by Harry W. Hazard, by permission of Princeton University Press.

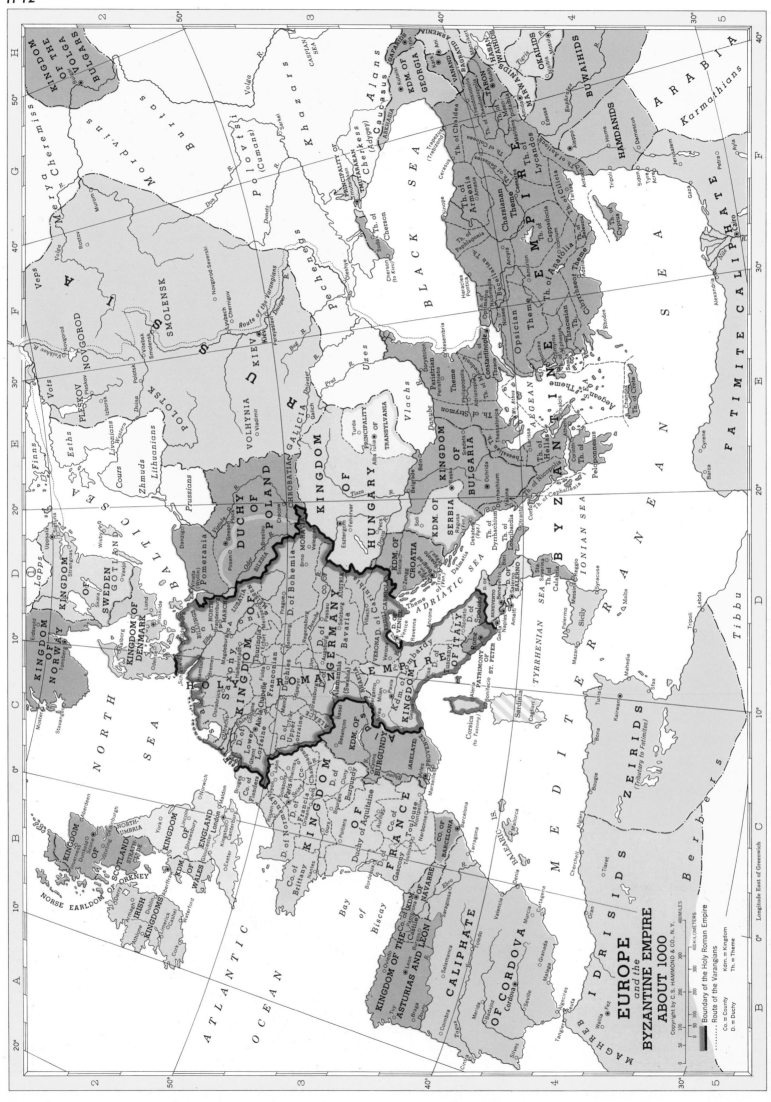

EUROPE
and the
BYZANTINE EMPIRE
ABOUT 1000

Copyright by C.S. HAMMOND & CO., N.Y.

——— Boundary of the Holy Roman Empire
········· Route of the Varangians

Co.= County   Kdm.= Kingdom
D.= Duchy   Th.= Theme

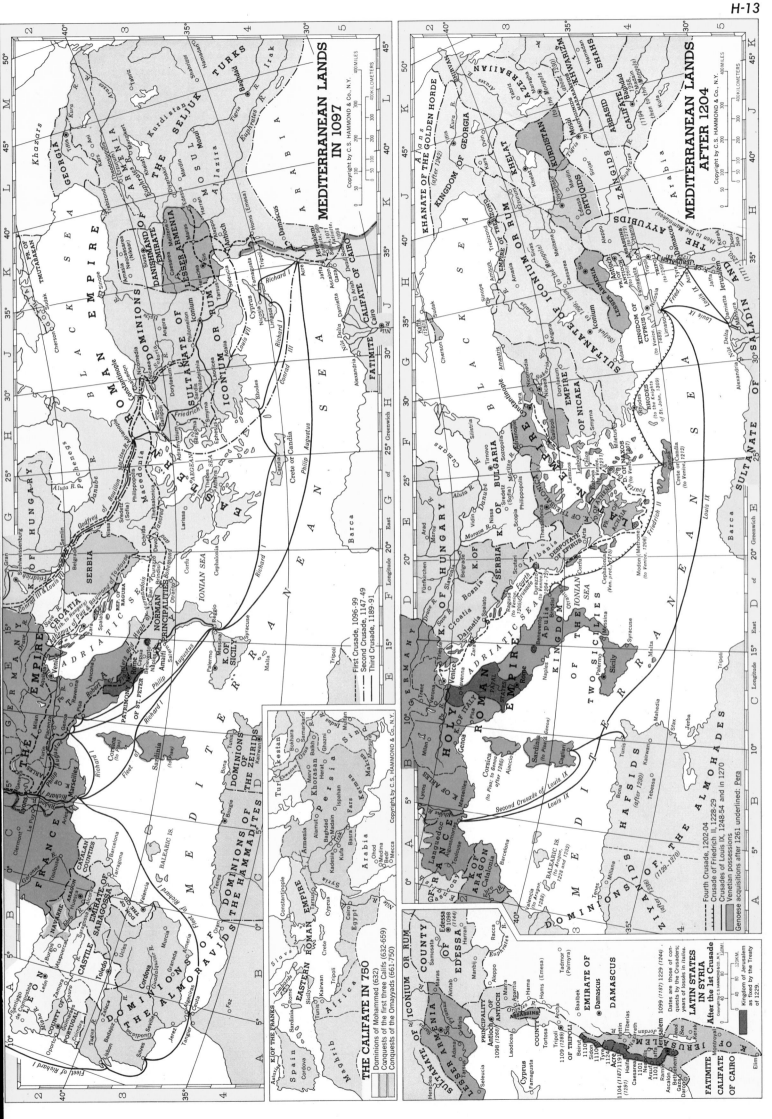

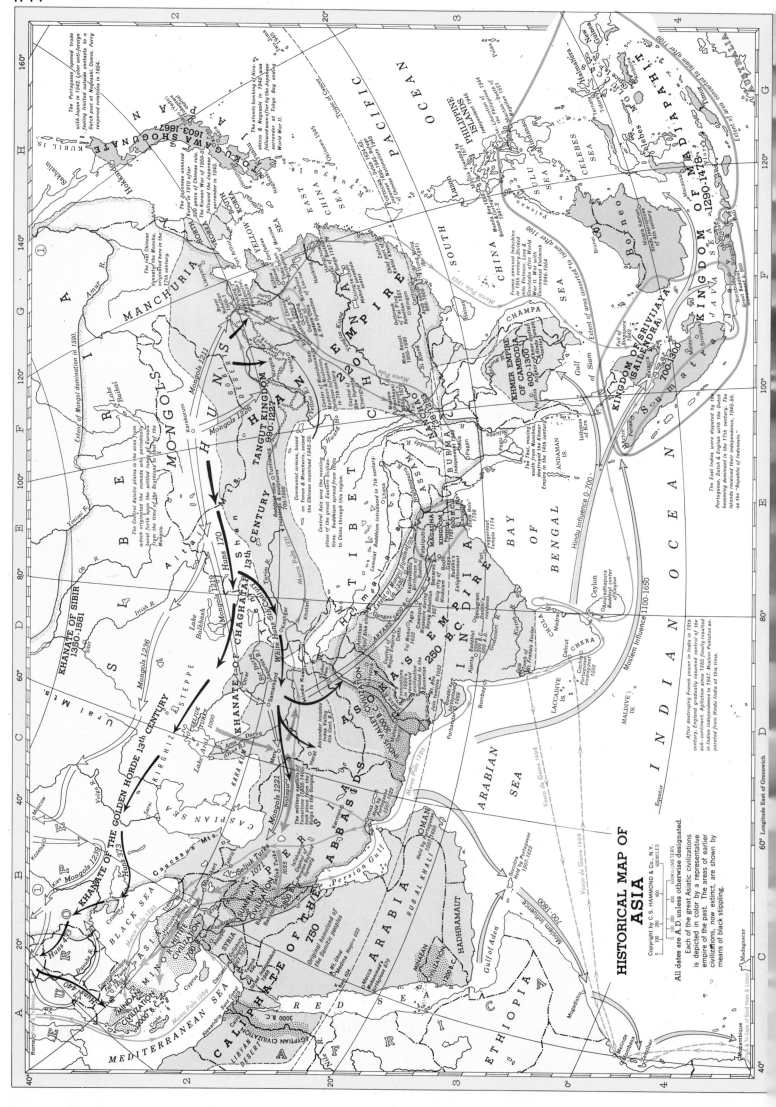

HISTORICAL MAP OF
ASIA

Copyright by C.S. HAMMOND & Co., N.Y.

All dates are A.D. unless otherwise designated.

Each of the great Asiatic civilizations
is depicted in color by a representative
empire of the past. The areas of earlier
civilizations, now extinct, are shown by
means of black stippling.

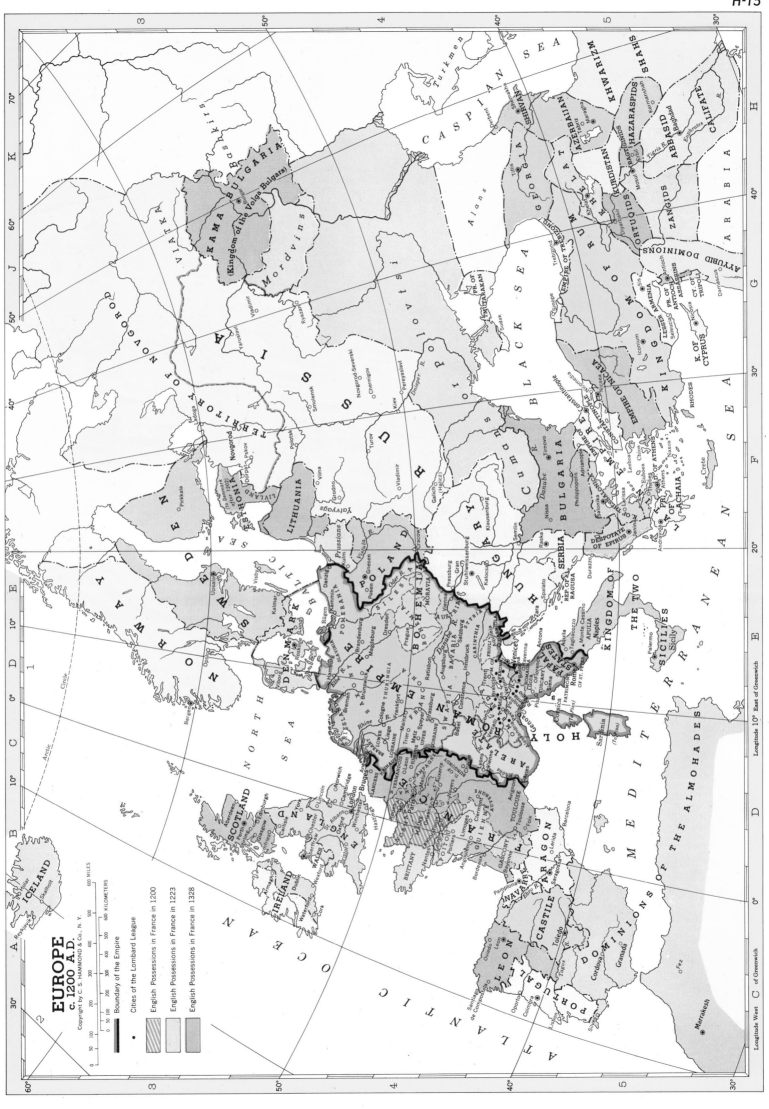

EUROPE
c. 1200 A.D.

Copyright by C. S. HAMMOND & Co., N.Y.

Boundary of the Empire

• Cities of the Lombard League

English Possessions in France in 1200

English Possessions in France in 1223

English Possessions in France in 1328

600 MILES

600 KILOMETERS

ECCLESIASTICAL MAP OF
EUROPE
c. 1300 A.D.

Archbishoprics
Bishoprics
Monasteries
Universities
The Archepiscopal provinces are colored

GREENLAND
Gardar
(To Trondjem)
Same scale as main map

C. S. HAMMOND & CO., N.Y.

Longitude   West   0°   East   of   Greenwich   10°   20°

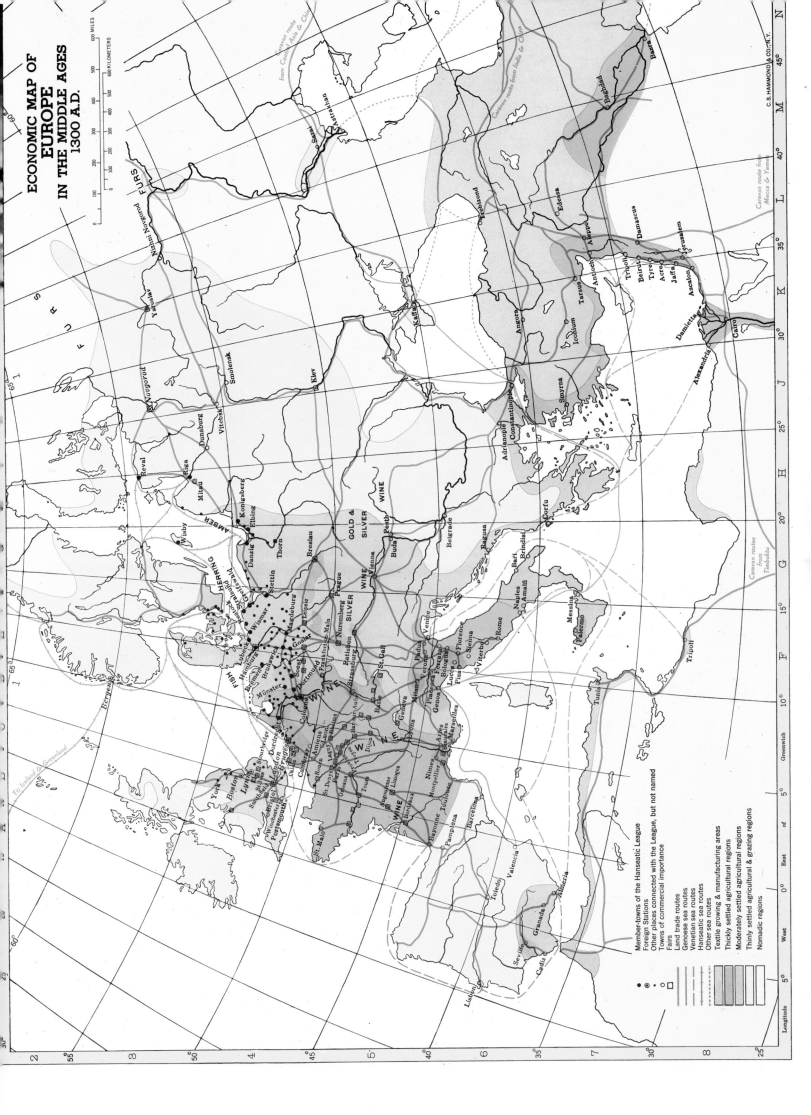

ECONOMIC MAP OF
EUROPE
IN THE MIDDLE AGES
1300 A.D.

C.S. HAMMOND & CO., N.Y.

Member-towns of the Hanseatic League
Foreign Stations
Other places connected with the League, but not named
Towns of commercial importance
Fairs
Land trade routes
Genoese sea routes
Venetian sea routes
Hanseatic sea routes
Other sea routes
Textile growing & manufacturing areas
Thickly settled agricultural regions
Moderately settled agricultural regions
Thinly settled agricultural & grazing regions
Nomadic regions

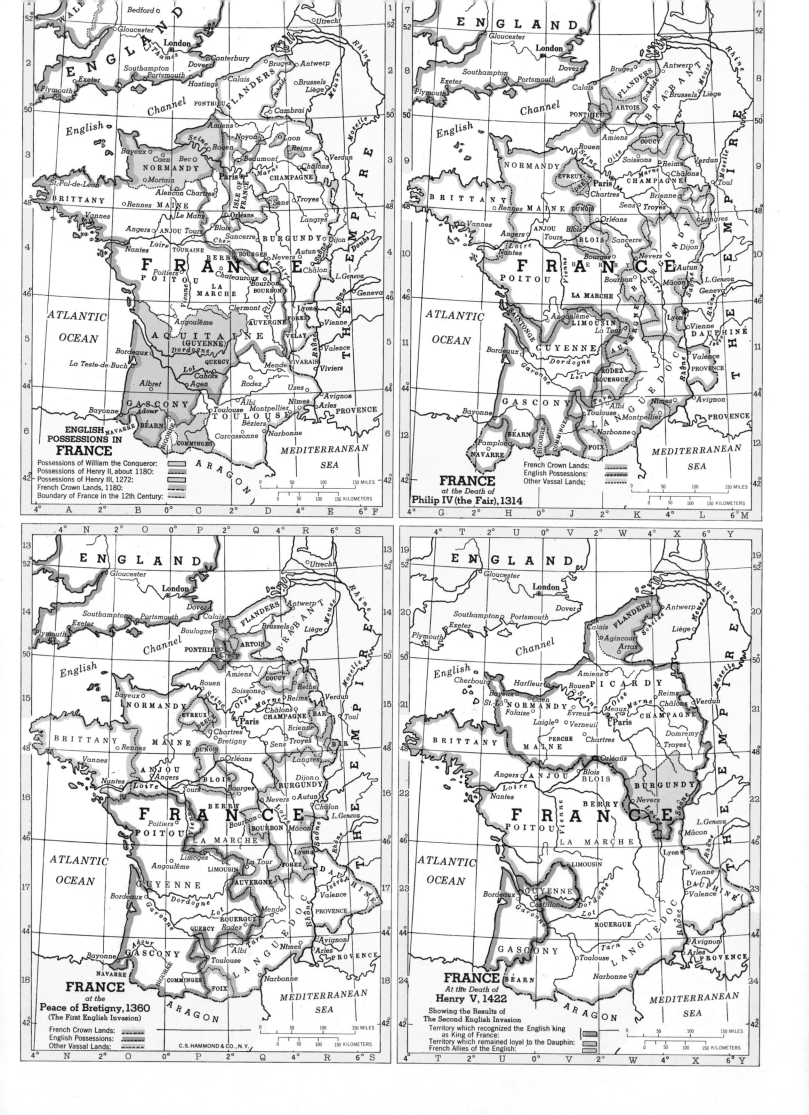

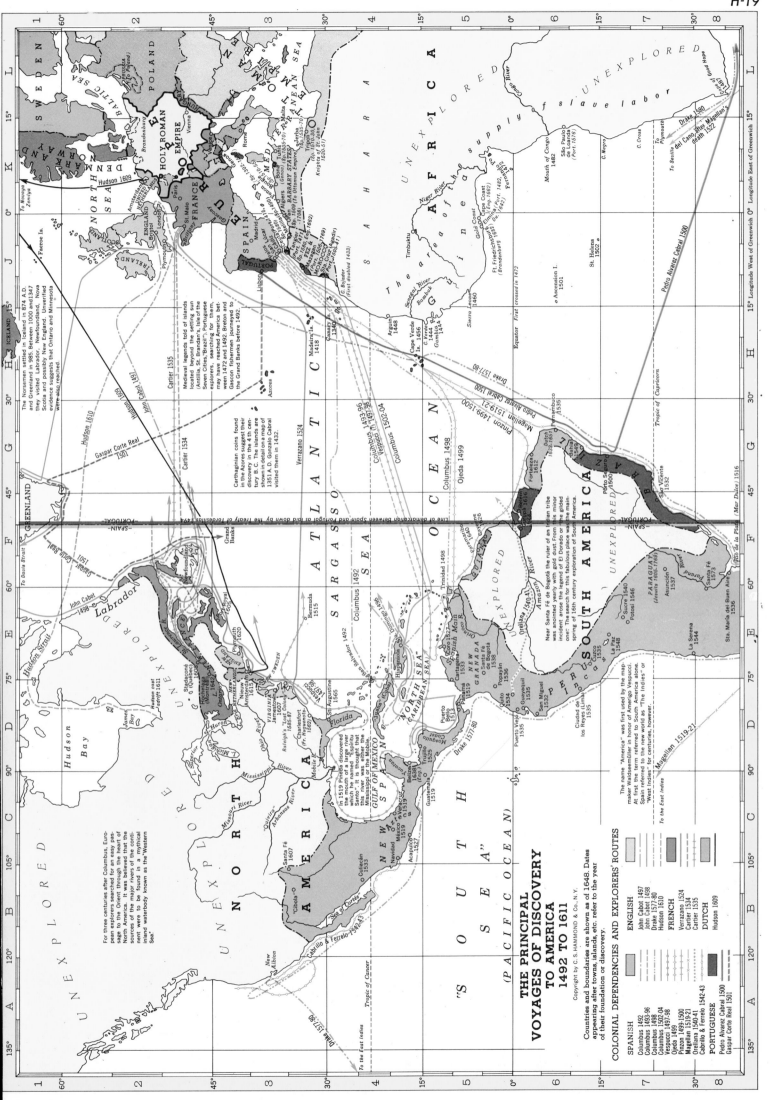

THE PRINCIPAL
VOYAGES OF DISCOVERY
TO AMERICA
1492 TO 1611

Copyright by C. S. HAMMOND & Co., N.Y.

Countries and boundaries are shown as of 1648. Dates
appearing after towns, islands, etc. refer to the year
of their foundation or discovery.

COLONIAL DEPENDENCIES AND EXPLORERS' ROUTES

SPANISH
Columbus 1492
Columbus 1493-96
Columbus 1498
Columbus 1502-04
Vespuci 1497-98
Ojeda 1499
Pinzon 1499-1500
Magellan 1519-21
Orellana 1540-41
Cabrillo & Ferrelo 1542-43

PORTUGUESE
Pedro Alvarez Cabral 1500
Gaspar Corte Real 1501

ENGLISH
John Cabot 1497
John Cabot 1498
Drake 1577-80
Hudson 1610

FRENCH
Verrazano 1524
Cartier 1534
Cartier 1535

DUTCH
Hudson 1609

The Norsemen settled in Iceland in 874 A.D.
and Greenland in 985. Between 1000 and 1347
they visited Labrador, Newfoundland, Nova
Scotia and possibly New England. Unverified
evidence suggests that Ontario and Minnesota
were also reached.

For three centuries after Columbus, European explorers searched for an easy pas-
sage to the Orient through the heart of
North America. It was believed that the
sources of the major rivers of the conti-
nent were to be found in a mythical
inland waterbody known as the "Western
Sea."

Medieval legends told of islands
located beyond the setting sun
(Antilia, St. Brandan's, Isle of the
Seven Cities, "Brazil"). Portuguese
explorers, searching for them,
may have reached America between 1472 and 1492. Breton and
Gascon fishermen journeyed to
the Grand Banks before 1492.

Carthaginian coins found
in the Azores suggest their
discovery in the 4 th century B.C. The islands are
shown in detail on a map of
1351 A.D. Gonzalo Cabral
visited them in 1432.

In 1519 Pineda discovered
the mouth of a large river
which he named Espiritu
Santo". It is thought that
this river was either the
Mississippi or the Mobile.

Near Santa Fé de Bogotá the ruler of an Indian tribe
was anointed yearly with gold dust. From this minor
incident arose the legend of El Dorado or the gilded
one". The search for this fabulous place was the main-
spring of 16th century exploration of South America.

The name "America" was first used by the map-
maker Waldseemüller in honor of Amerigo Vespucci.
At first the term referred to South America alone.
Spain referred to the new world as "The Indies" or
"West Indies" for centuries, however.

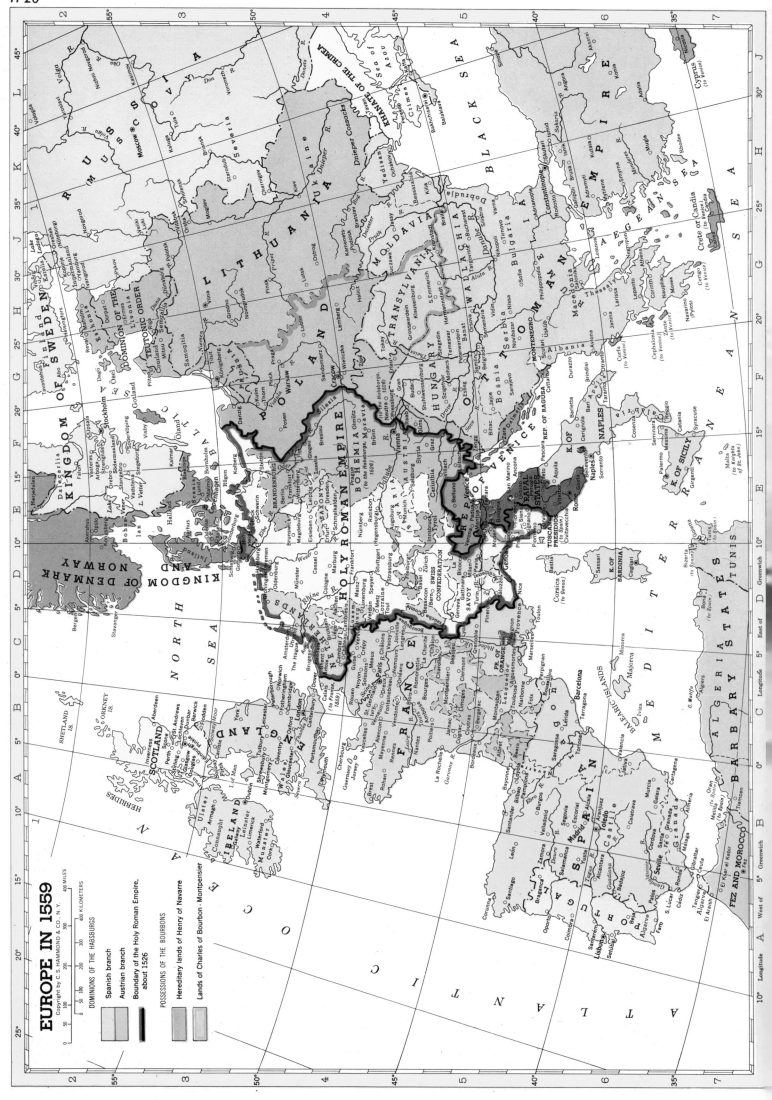

EUROPE IN 1559

Copyright by C. S. HAMMOND & CO., N.Y.

DOMINIONS OF THE HABSBURGS

Spanish branch

Austrian branch

Boundary of the Holy Roman Empire, about 1526

POSSESSIONS OF THE BOURBONS

Hereditary lands of Henry of Navarre

Lands of Charles of Bourbon-Montpensier

EUROPE IN 1648
AT THE PEACE OF WESTPHALIA

Copyright by C. S. HAMMOND & CO., N.Y.

Boundary of the Empire

Church Lands

Transylvania, independent of
Hungarian Kingdom with Turkish
Backing.

DOMINIONS OF THE HABSBURGS

Spanish Branch

Austrian Branch

50 0 100 200 300 400 MILES
0 50 100 200 300 400 KILOMETERS

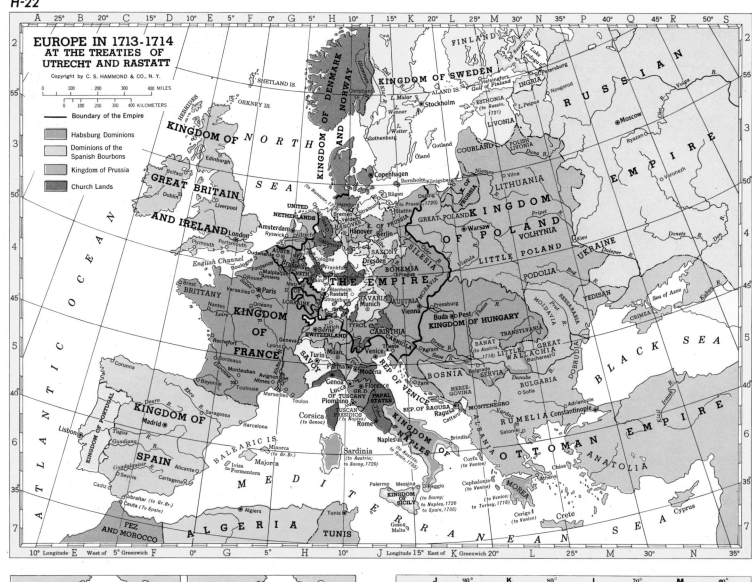

EUROPE IN 1713-1714
AT THE TREATIES OF UTRECHT AND RASTATT

Copyright by C. S. HAMMOND & CO., N. Y.

	Boundary of the Empire
	Habsburg Dominions
	Dominions of the Spanish Bourbons
	Kingdom of Prussia
	Church Lands

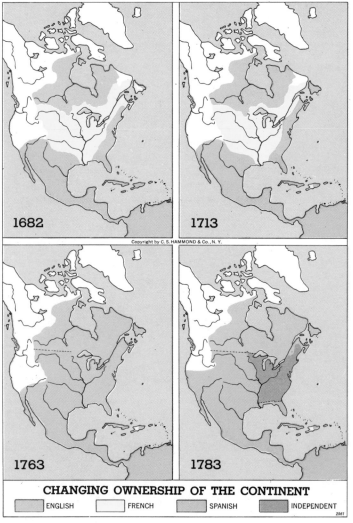

1682

1713

1763

1783

CHANGING OWNERSHIP OF THE CONTINENT

ENGLISH FRENCH SPANISH INDEPENDENT

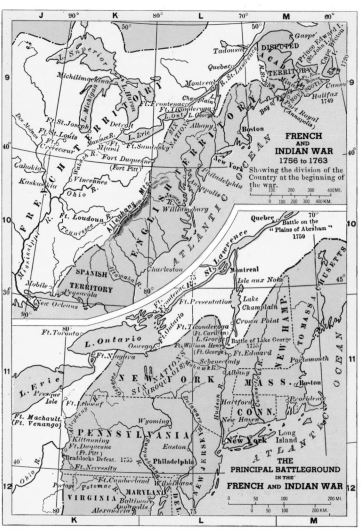

FRENCH AND INDIAN WAR
1756 to 1763

Showing the division of the Country at the beginning of the war.

THE PRINCIPAL BATTLEGROUND IN THE FRENCH AND INDIAN WAR

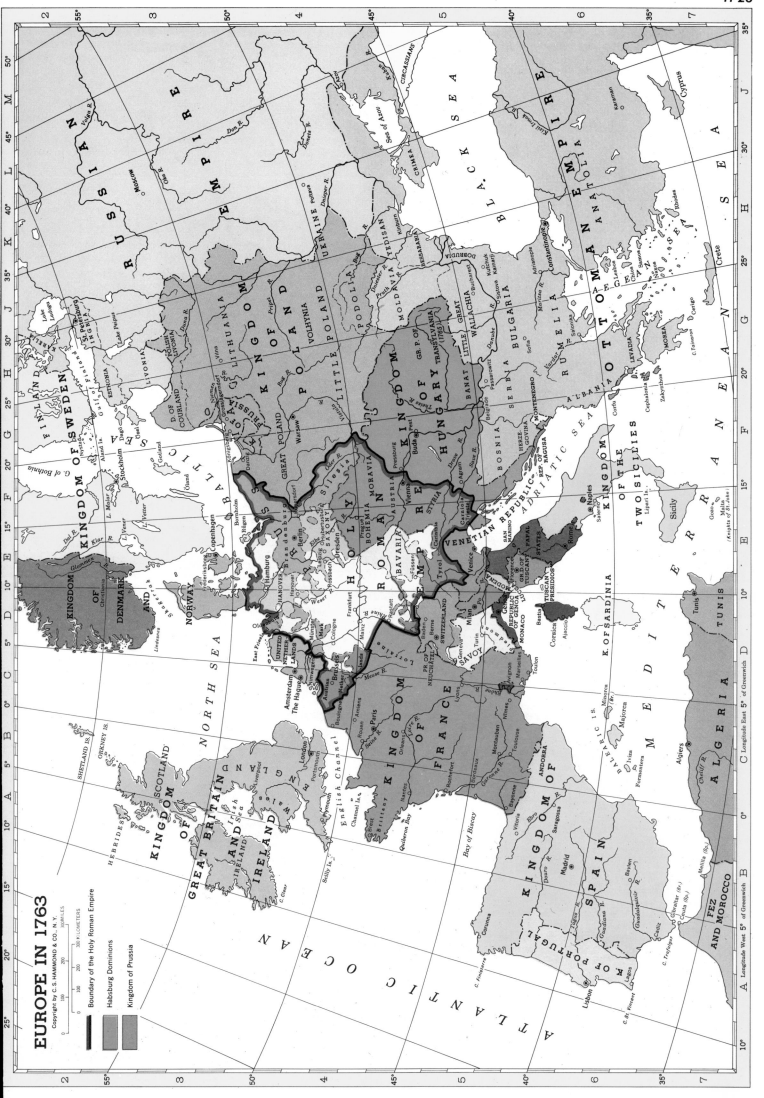

EUROPE IN 1763

Copyright by C. S. HAMMOND & CO., N.Y.

Boundary of the Holy Roman Empire

Habsburg Dominions

Kingdom of Prussia

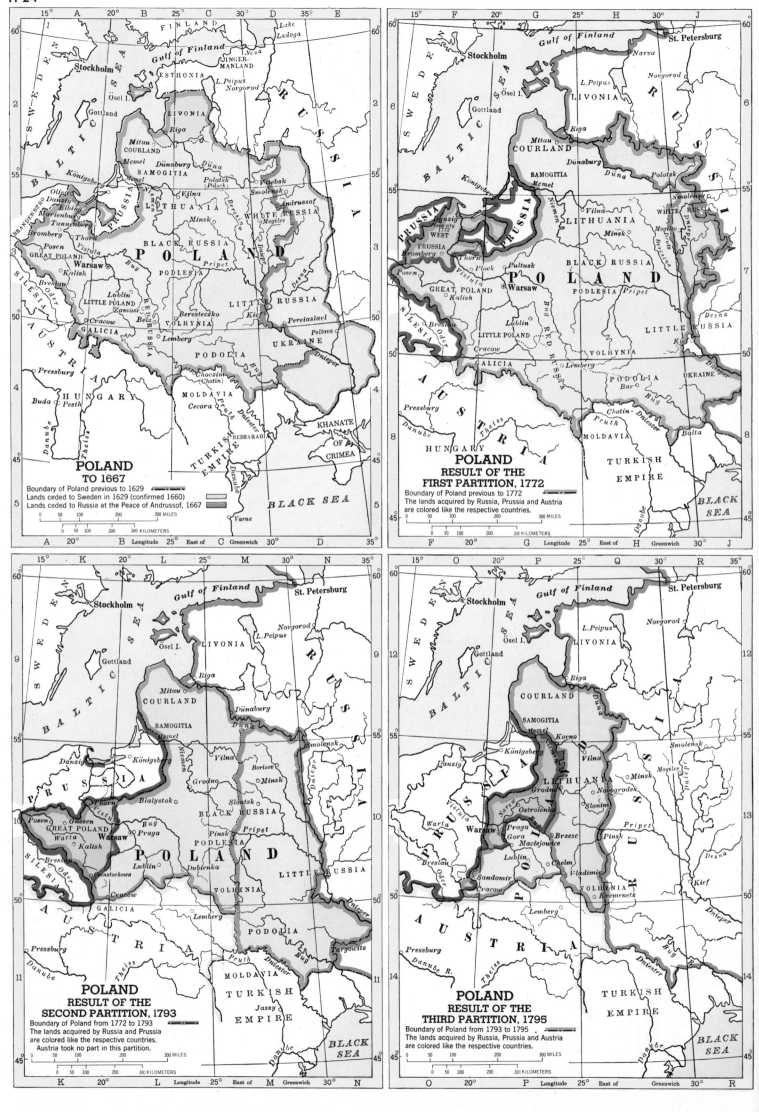

POLAND
TO 1667

Boundary of Poland previous to 1629
Lands ceded to Sweden in 1629 (confirmed 1660)
Lands ceded to Russia at the Peace of Andrussof, 1667

0   50   100   200   300 MILES
0   50 100   200   300 KILOMETERS

POLAND
RESULT OF THE
FIRST PARTITION, 1772

Boundary of Poland previous to 1772
The lands acquired by Russia, Prussia and Austria
are colored like the respective countries.

0   50   100   200   300 MILES
0   50 100   200   300 KILOMETERS

POLAND
RESULT OF THE
SECOND PARTITION, 1793

Boundary of Poland from 1772 to 1793
The lands acquired by Russia and Prussia
are colored like the respective countries.
Austria took no part in this partition.

0   50   100   200   300 MILES
0   50 100   200   300 KILOMETERS

POLAND
RESULT OF THE
THIRD PARTITION, 1795

Boundary of Poland from 1793 to 1795
The lands acquired by Russia, Prussia and Austria
are colored like the respective countries.

0   50   100   200   300 MILES
0   50 100   200   300 KILOMETERS

FRANCE
AT THE OUTBREAK OF THE
REVOLUTION
INEQUALITIES OF THE SALT TAX

0   25   50   100   150   200 MILES

0 25 50 100   150   200 KILOMETERS

Region of the great salt tax (grande gabelle)
Region of the little salt tax (petite gabelle)
Region of other low rates
Region of the "redeemed provinces"
Region of the "free provinces"
The figures show the relative prices paid for a certain amount of salt in various parts of France.
"Provinces d'étranger effectif" (i. e. acquired since 1664, or endowed with special privileges)
B. Bishopric.   C. County.

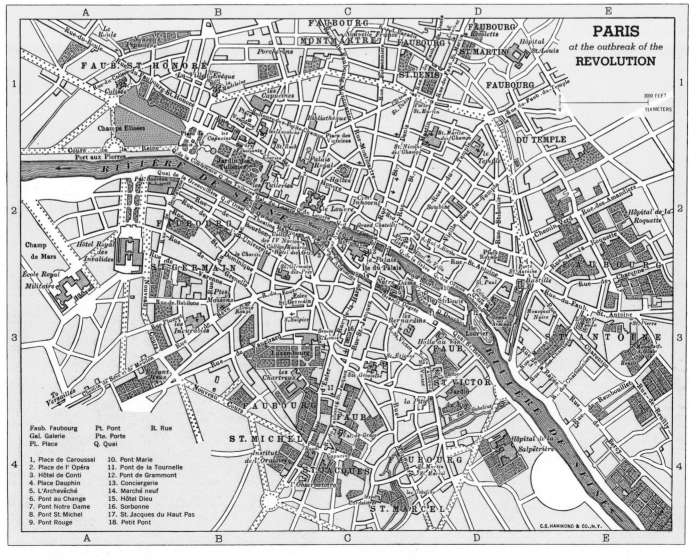

PARIS
at the outbreak of the
REVOLUTION

0   3000 FEET
914 METERS

Faub. Faubourg   Pt. Pont   R. Rue
Gal. Galerie   Pte. Porte
Pl. Place   Q. Quai

1, Place de Caroussel   10. Pont Marie
2. Place de l' Opéra   11. Pont de la Tournelle
3. Hôtel de Conti   12. Pont de Grammont
4. Place Dauphin   13. Conciergerie
5. L'Archevêché   14. Marché neuf
6. Pont au Change   15. Hôtel Dieu
7. Pont Notre Dame   16. Sorbonne
8. Pont St. Michel   17. St. Jacques du Haut Pas
9. Pont Rouge   18. Petit Pont

C.S. HAMMOND & CO., N.Y.

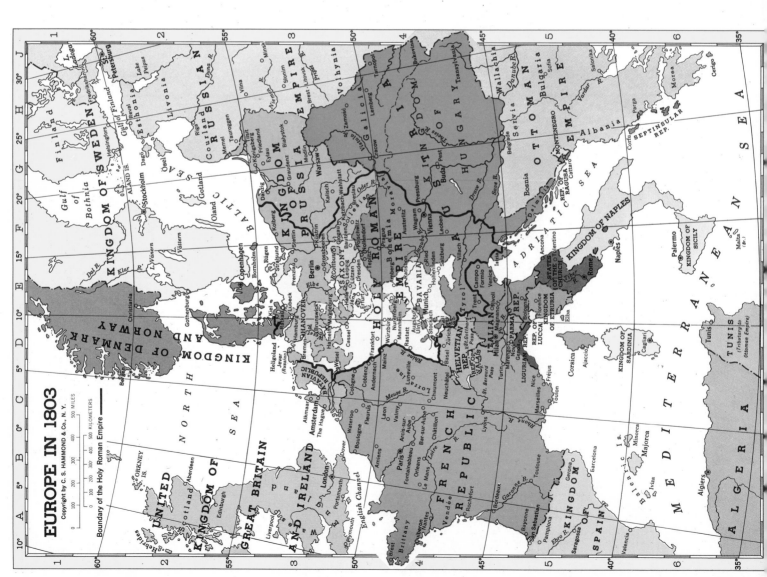

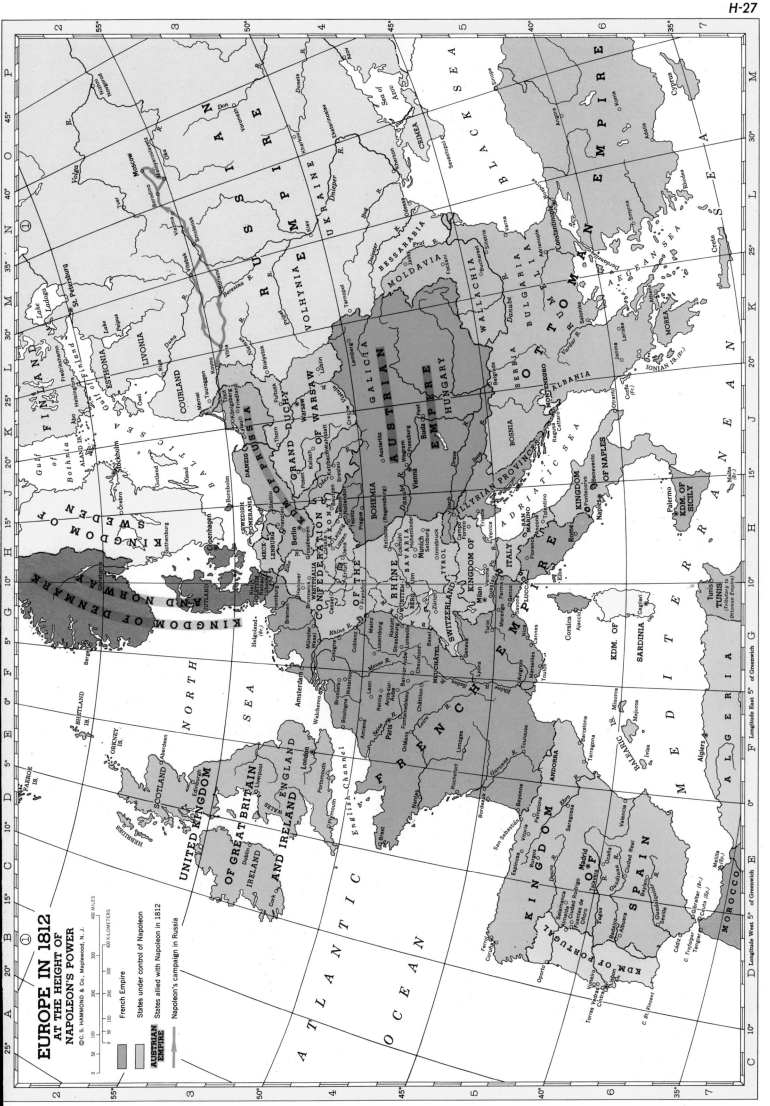

EUROPE IN 1812
AT THE HEIGHT OF NAPOLEON'S POWER

©C. S. HAMMOND & CO., Maplewood, N. J.

Legend:
- French Empire
- States under control of Napoleon in 1812
- States allied with Napoleon in 1812
- Napoleon's campaign in Russia

AUSTRIAN EMPIRE

Scale:
MILES — 0 50 100 200 300 400 MILES
KILOMETERS — 0 100 200 300 400 KILOMETERS

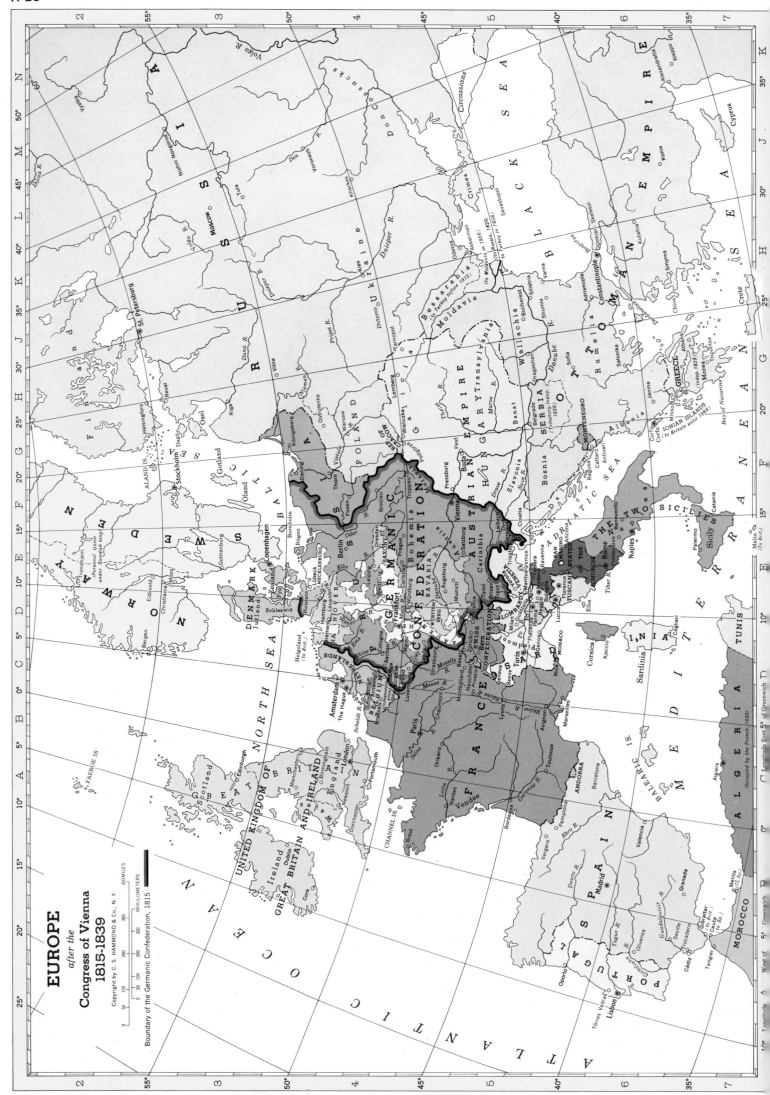

EUROPE
after the
Congress of Vienna
1815-1839

Copyright by C. S. HAMMOND & Co. N. Y.

Boundary of the Germanic Confederation, 1815

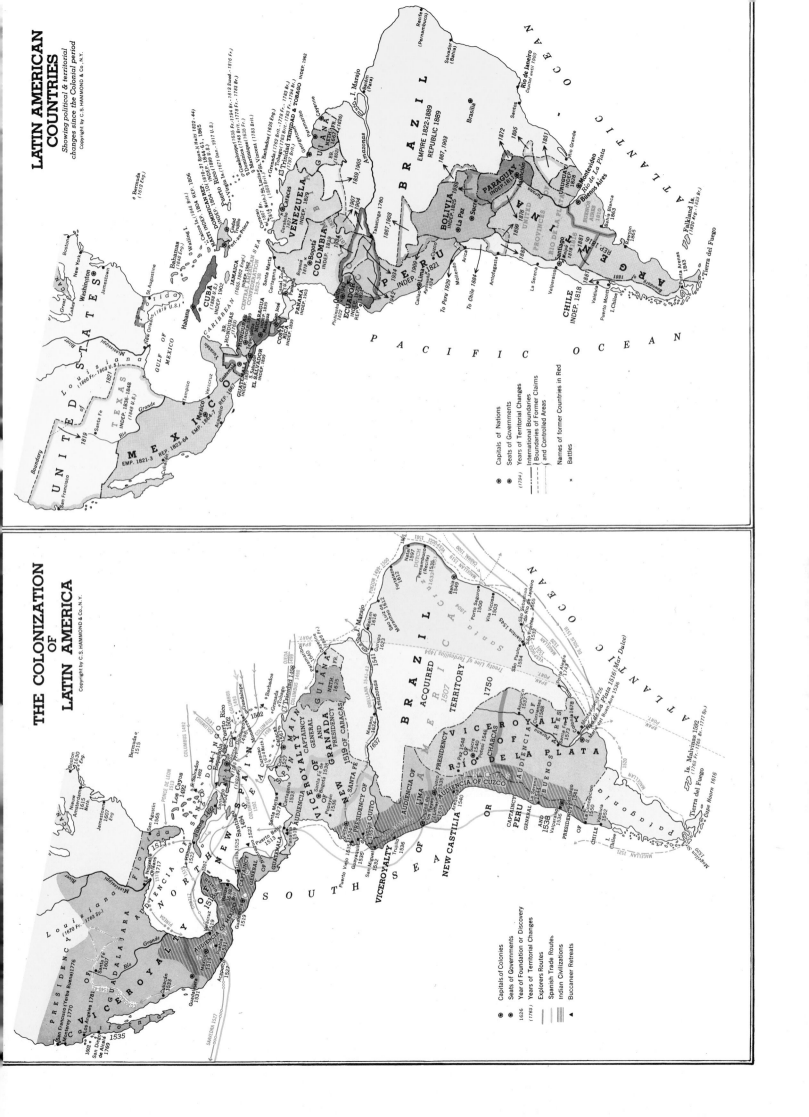

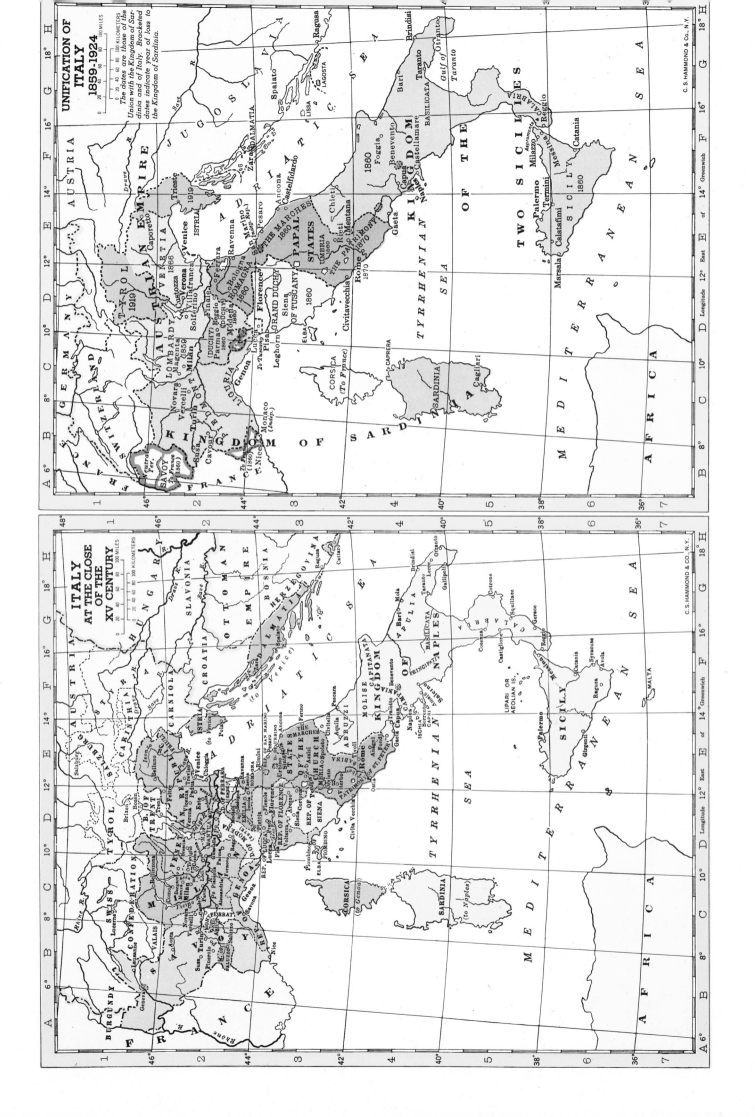

C. S. HAMMOND & Co., N.Y.

UNIFICATION OF ITALY 1859-1924

The dates are those of the Union with the Kingdom of Sardinia and of Italy. Bracketed dates indicate year of loss to the Kingdom of Sardinia.

SCALE OF MILES
0   20   40   60   80   100 MILES
SCALE OF KILOMETERS
0   20   40   60   80   100 KILOMETERS

Left map (Unification of Italy 1859-1924)

AUSTRIA

GERMANY

SWITZERLAND

FRANCE

JUGOSLAVIA

AUSTRIAN EMPIRE

T-YROL 1919

Caporetto

Trieste 1919

VENETIA 1866

ISTRIA 1919

Venice 1866

Custozza 1866

Verona

Villafranca

Solferino (1859)

Magenta (1859)

LOMBARDY 1859

Milan

Novara

Vercelli

PIEDMONT

Turin

Susa

Cavour

E.Nice

Monaco (Indep.)

To France (1860)

SAVOY

Neutral Ter.

To France (1860)

KINGDOM OF SARDINIA

LIGURIA

Genoa

GRAND DUCHY OF TUSCANY

Florence 1860

Siena

Leghorn

Pisa

Lucca

ELBA

DUCHY OF PARMA 1860

Finale

Parma

Reggio

MODENA (DUCHY) 1860

Bologna

ROMAGNA 1860

Ferrara

Ravenna

San Marino (Indep. Rep.)

Pesaro

THE MARCHES 1860

Ancona

Castelfidardo

ADRIATIC SEA

Zara DALMATIA

Spalato

LAGOSTA

LISSA

Ragusa

UMBRIA 1860

PAPAL STATES

Rieti

Chieti

Mentana

Civitavecchia

Rome 1870

THE PATRIMONY 1870

Gaeta

CORSICA (To France)

CAPRERA

SARDINIA

Cagliari

TYRRHENIAN SEA

MEDITERRANEAN SEA

AFRICA

KINGDOM OF THE TWO SICILIES

1860

Foggia

Benevento

Capua

Naples

Castellammare

Bari

Taranto

Gulf of Taranto

Brindisi

BASILICATA

CALABRIA

Aspromonte

Milazzo

Messina

Reggio

Palermo

Termini

SICILY 1860

Marsala

Calatafimi

Catania

C. S. HAMMOND & Co., N.Y.

Right map (Italy at the Close of the XV Century)

ITALY AT THE CLOSE OF THE XV CENTURY

SCALE OF MILES
0   20   40   60   80   100 MILES
SCALE OF KILOMETERS
0   20   40   60   80   100 KILOMETERS

AUSTRIA

HUNGARY

SALZBURG

Salzburg

TYROL

Brixen

Bozen

STYRIA

CARINTHIA

CARNIOLA

CROATIA

SLAVONIA

BOSNIA

HERZEGOVINA

DALMATIA (to Venice)

Spalato

Ragusa

Cattaro

OTTOMAN EMPIRE

SWISS CONFEDERATION

Lucerne

Lausanne

Geneva

VALAIS

BURGUNDY

FRANCE

Rhône R.

Nice

SAVOY

MONFERRAT

Susa

Turin

Pinerolo

Saluzzo

SALUZZO

MARQ. OF MONTFERRAT

MILAN

Milan

Como

Bergamo

Brescia

MANTUA

REP. OF VENICE

Venice

Belluno

Feltre

Trento

B. OF TRENT

Verona

Vicenza

Padua

Chioggia

Este

D. OF FERRARA

Ferrara

Ravenna

Rimini

REP. OF SAN MARINO

THE MARCHES

Pesaro

Urbino

D. OF URBINO

Ancona

Ferno

Pescara

Aquila

ABRUZZI

Civitella

CHURCH STATES OF THE

Spoleto

UMBRIA

Assisi

Perugia

REP. OF PERUGIA

Orvieto

PATRIMONY OF ST. PETER

Viterbo

Rome

Tivoli

Anagni

Fondi

MODENA

Modena

Reggio

Parma

D. OF MODENA

EMILIA

Bologna

Imola

Faenza

Forli

REP. OF LUCCA

Lucca

REP. OF FLORENCE

Florence

Fiesole

Pistoia

Pisa

PISA

Volterra

SIENA

Siena

Cortona

Arezzo

Chiusi

GENOA

Genoa

Savona

Piombino

ELBA

CORSICA (to Genoa)

Civita Vecchia

Ostia

ADRIATIC SEA

TYRRHENIAN SEA

SARDINIA (to Naples)

KINGDOM OF NAPLES

MOLISE

CAPITANATA

PRINCIPATO

Benevento

Trajetto

Gaeta

Capua

ISCHIA

Naples

Sorrento

CAPRI

SALERNO

Salerno

APULIA

Bari

Mola

Taranto

Lecce

Gallipoli

Otranto

Brindisi

BASILICATA

CALABRIA

Cosenza

Castiglione

Squillace

Gerace

Cotrone

Reggio

Messina

LIPARI OR AEOLIAN IS.

SICILY

Palermo

Girgenti

Catania

Syracuse

Avola

Ragusa

MALTA

MEDITERRANEAN SEA

AFRICA

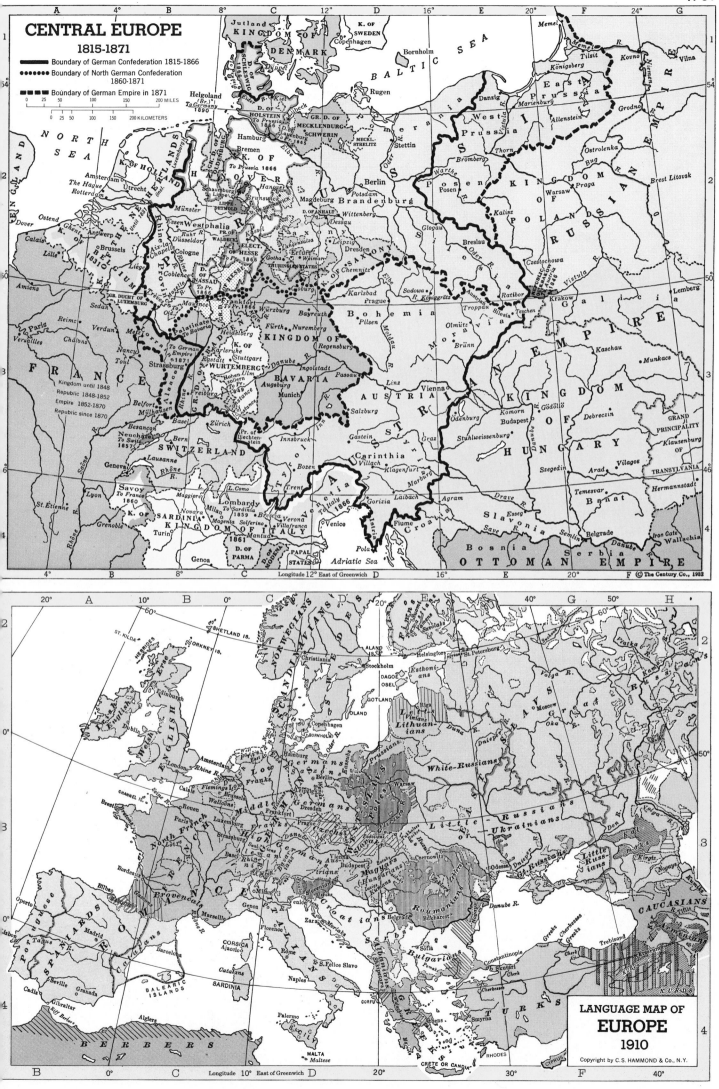

CENTRAL EUROPE
1815-1871

━━━━ Boundary of German Confederation 1815-1866
●●●●● Boundary of North German Confederation 1860-1871
▄▄▄▄ Boundary of German Empire in 1871

Longitude 12° East of Greenwich

© The Century Co., 1932

LANGUAGE MAP OF
EUROPE
1910

Copyright by C.S. Hammond & Co., N.Y.

Longitude 10° East of Greenwich

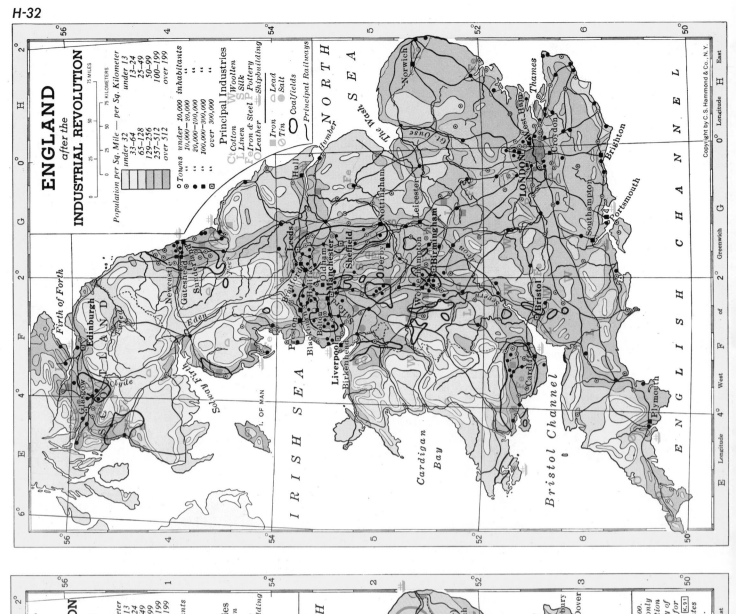

ENGLAND
after the
INDUSTRIAL REVOLUTION

Population per Sq. Mile — per Sq. Kilometer

under 32	under 13
33–64	13–24
65–128	25–49
129–256	50–99
257–512	100–199
over 512	over 199

Towns under 10,000 inhabitants ○
10,000–20,000 ⊙
20,000–100,000 ●
100,000–300,000 ⊡
over 300,000 ▣

Principal Industries
Ct Cotton W Woollen
L Linen S Silk
Fe Iron & Steel P Pottery
○ Leather Shipbuilding

■ Lead □ Salt
◆ Iron ● Tin
○ Coalfields Principal Railways

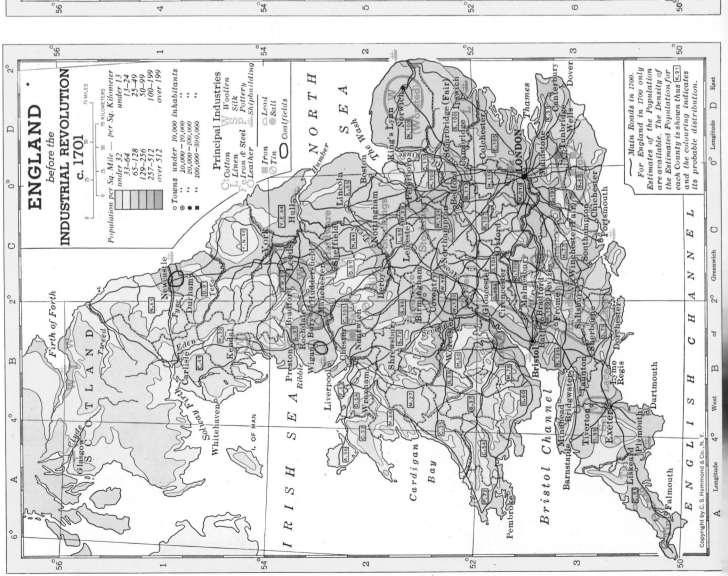

ENGLAND
before the
INDUSTRIAL REVOLUTION
c. 1701

Population per Sq. Mile — per Sq. Kilometer

under 32	under 13
33–64	13–24
65–128	25–49
129–256	50–99
257–512	100–199
	over 512	100,000–300,000

Towns under 10,000 inhabitants ○
10,000–20,000 ⊙
20,000–100,000 ●
100,000–300,000 ■

Principal Industries
Ct Cotton W Woollen
L Linen S Silk
Fe Iron & Steel P Pottery
○ Leather Shipbuilding

■ Lead □ Salt
◆ Iron ● Tin
○ Coalfields

— Main Roads in 1700.
For England in 1700 only
Estimates of the Population
are available. The Density of
the Estimated Population for
each County is shown thus [K.91]
and the colouring indicates
its probable distribution.

Copyright by C. S. Hammond & Co., N. Y.

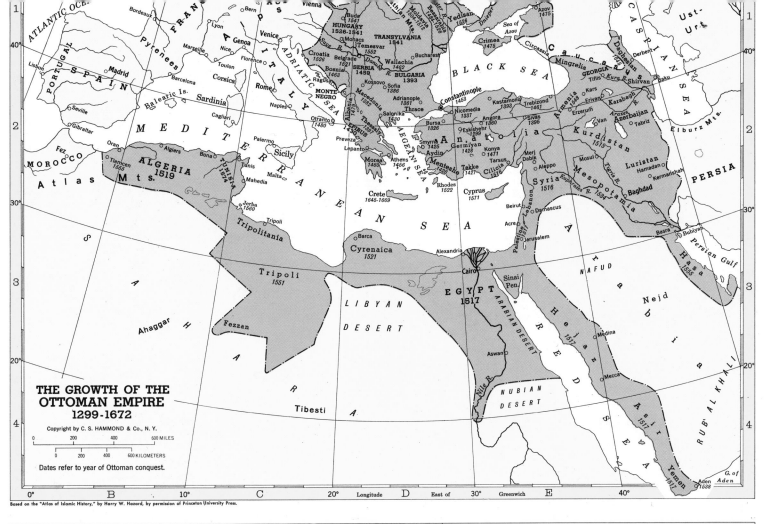

THE GROWTH OF THE OTTOMAN EMPIRE 1299-1672

Copyright by C. S. HAMMOND & Co., N. Y.

0   200   400   600 MILES

0   200   400   600 KILOMETERS

Dates refer to year of Ottoman conquest.

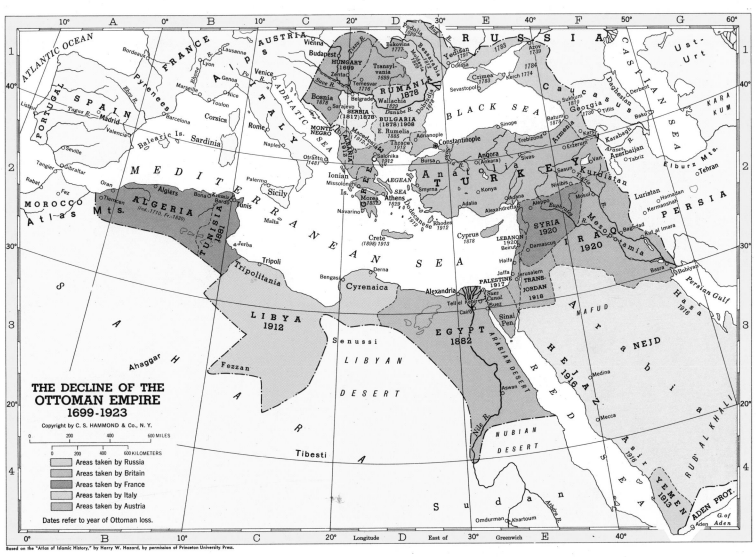

THE DECLINE OF THE OTTOMAN EMPIRE 1699-1923

Copyright by C. S. HAMMOND & Co., N. Y.

0   200   400   600 MILES

0   200   400   600 KILOMETERS

Areas taken by Russia
Areas taken by Britain
Areas taken by France
Areas taken by Italy
Areas taken by Austria

Dates refer to year of Ottoman loss.

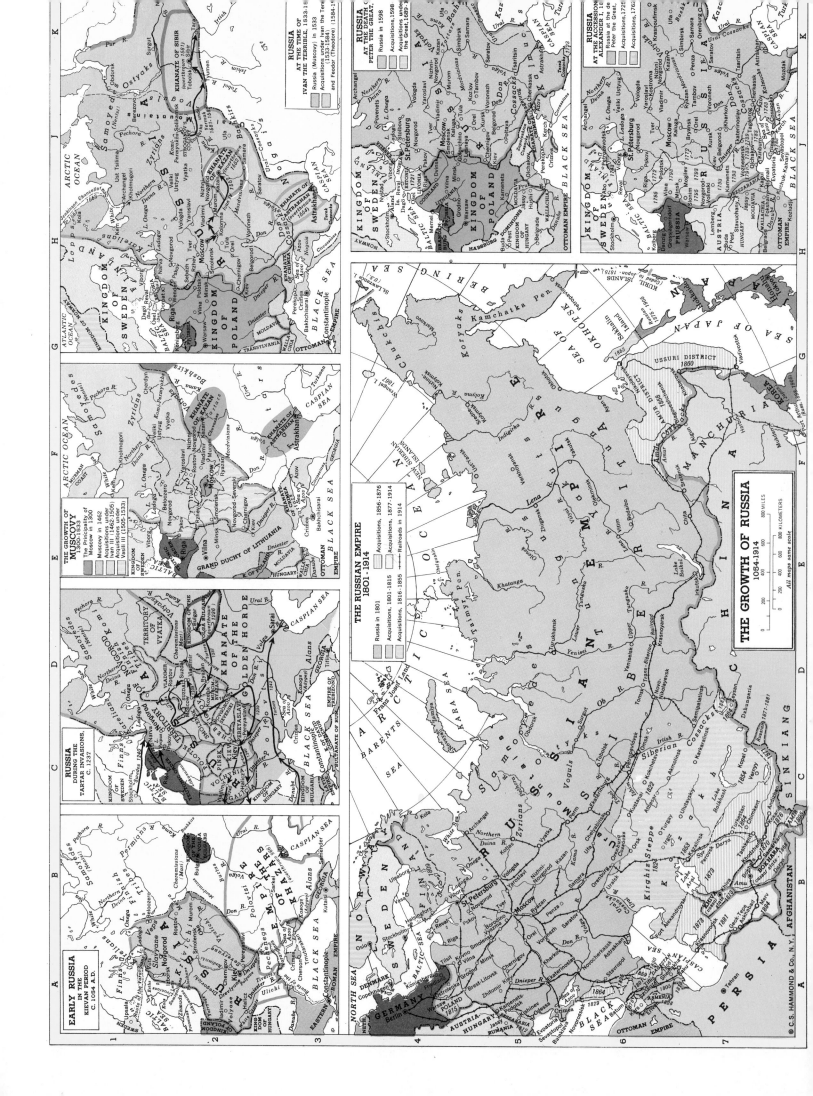

RUSSIA AT THE TIME OF IVAN THE TERRIBLE, 1533-15[...]

RUSSIA AT THE TIME OF IVAN THE TERRIBLE, 1533-15[...]
- Russia (Muscovy) in 1533
- Acquisitions under Ivan the Ter[...] (1533-1584)
- and Fedor (Theodore) (1584-[...])

RUSSIA AT THE DEATH O[...] PETER THE GREAT,
- Russia in 1598
- Acquisitions under [...] the Great, (1689-[...]

RUSSIA AT THE ACCESSIO[...] ALEXANDER I[...]
- Russia at the de[...] Peter the Great,
- Acquisitions under [...]

EARLY RUSSIA IN THE KIEVAN PERIOD C. 1054 A.D.

RUSSIA DURING THE TARTAR INVASIONS, C. 1237

THE GROWTH OF MUSCOVY 1300-1533
- The Principality of Moscow in 1300
- Muscovy in 1462
- Acquisitions under Ivan III (1462-1505)
- Acquisitions under Vasili III (1505-1533)

THE RUSSIAN EMPIRE 1801-1914
- Russia in 1801
- Acquisitions, 1801-1815
- Acquisitions, 1816-1855
- Acquisitions, 1856-1876
- Acquisitions, 1877-1914
- Railroads in 1914

THE GROWTH OF RUSSIA 1054-1914

0 200 400 600 800 MILES
0 200 400 600 800 KILOMETERS
All maps same scale

© C.S. HAMMOND & Co., N.Y.

ASIA IN 1914

Copyright by C. S. HAMMOND & Co., N.Y.

AFRICA IN 1914

Copyright by C. S. HAMMOND & Co., N.Y.

EUROPEAN POSSESSIONS

British · French · German · Italian · Portuguese · Spanish · Belgian

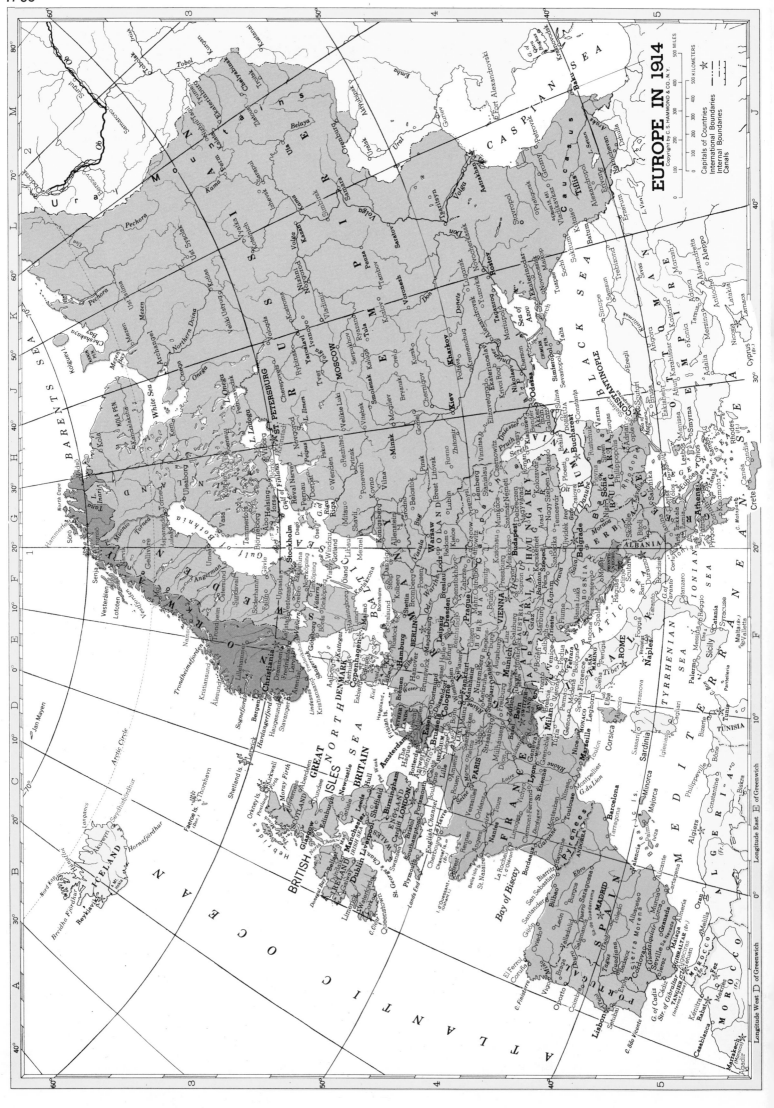

EUROPE IN 1914

Copyright by C. S. HAMMOND & CO., N.Y.

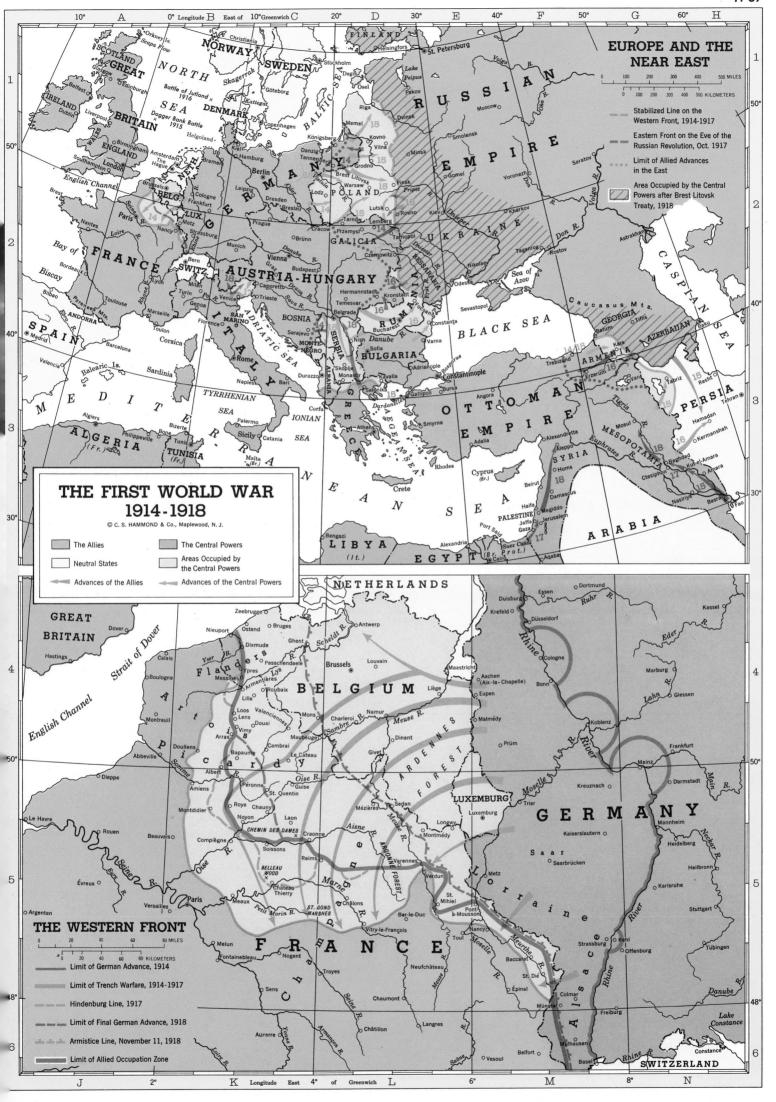

EUROPE AND THE NEAR EAST

| | 100 | 200 | 300 | 400 | 500 MILES |

Stabilized Line on the Western Front, 1914-1917

Eastern Front on the Eve of the Russian Revolution, Oct. 1917

Limit of Allied Advances in the East

Area Occupied by the Central Powers after Brest Litovsk Treaty, 1918

THE FIRST WORLD WAR
1914-1918

© C. S. HAMMOND & Co., Maplewood, N.J.

The Allies	The Central Powers
Neutral States	Areas Occupied by the Central Powers
Advances of the Allies	Advances of the Central Powers

THE WESTERN FRONT

| 0 | 20 | 40 | 60 | 80 MILES |
| 0 | 20 | 40 | 60 | 80 KILOMETERS |

Limit of German Advance, 1914

Limit of Trench Warfare, 1914-1917

Hindenburg Line, 1917

Limit of Final German Advance, 1918

Armistice Line, November 11, 1918

Limit of Allied Occupation Zone

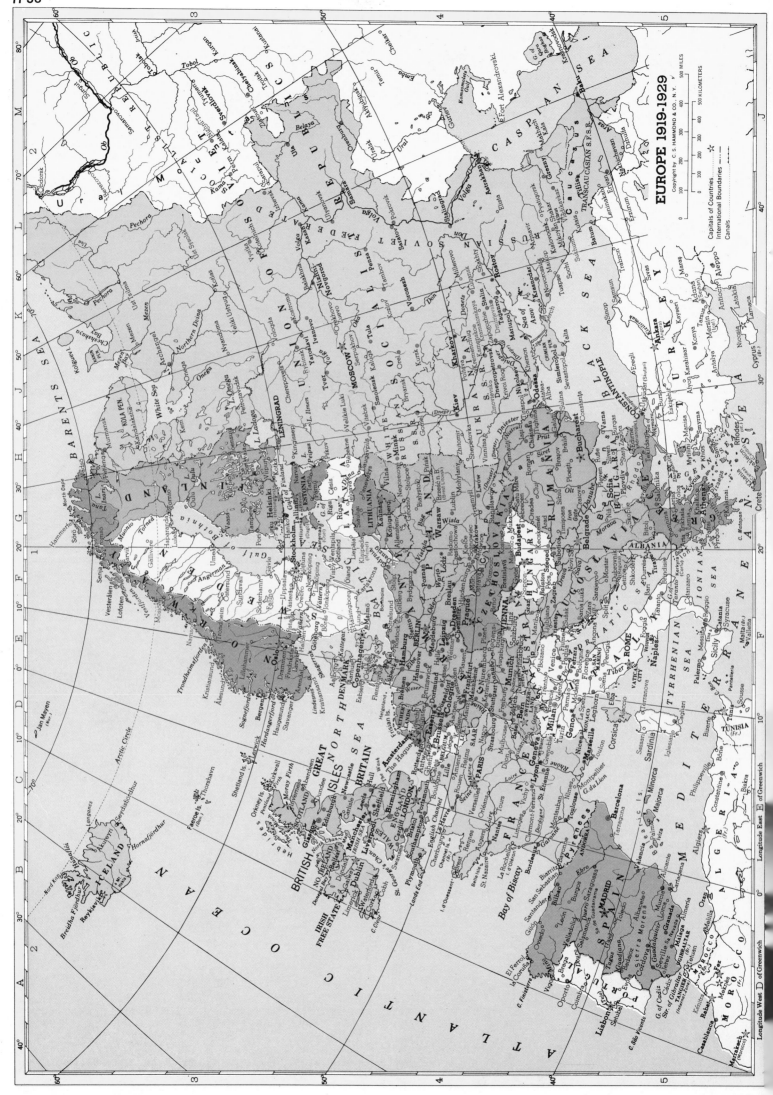

EUROPE 1919-1929

Copyright by C. S. HAMMOND & CO., N. Y.

Capitals of Countries .... ✯
International Boundaries ....
Canals ....

| 0 | 100 | 200 | 300 | 400 | 500 MILES |
| 0 | 100 | 200 | 300 | 400 | 500 KILOMETERS |

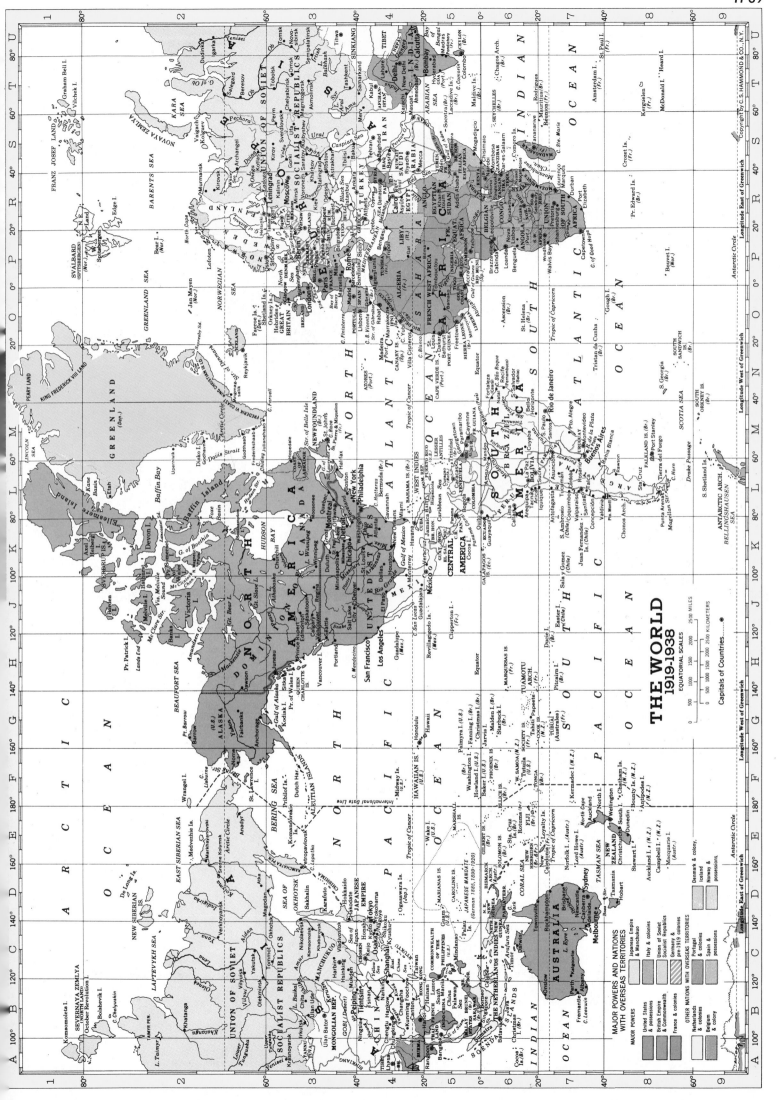

THE WORLD
1919-1938

EQUATORIAL SCALES

Capitals of Countries...... ●

MAJOR POWERS AND NATIONS
WITH OVERSEAS TERRITORIES

MAJOR POWERS

United States & possessions
Italy & colonies
Union of Soviet Socialist Republics
British Empire & Commonwealth
Germany pre-1919 colonies
France & colonies
Japanese Empire & Manchukuo

OTHER NATIONS WITH OVERSEAS TERRITORIES

Netherlands & colonies
Portugal & colonies
Belgium & colony
Spain & possessions

Denmark & colony
Iceland
Norway & possessions

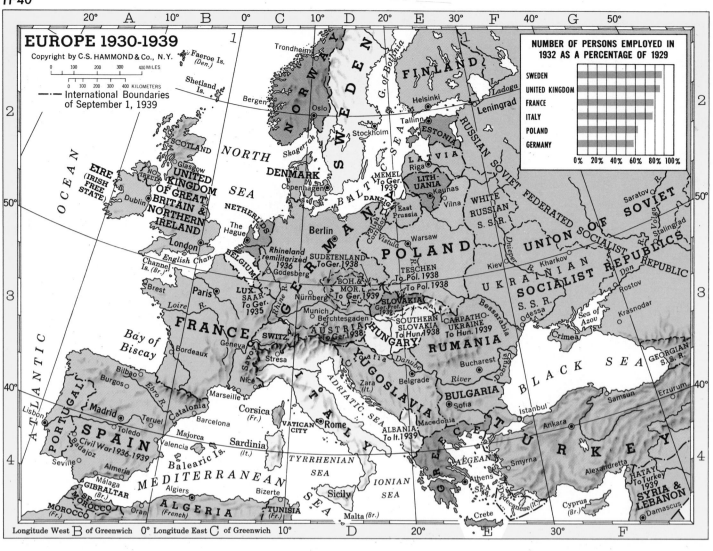

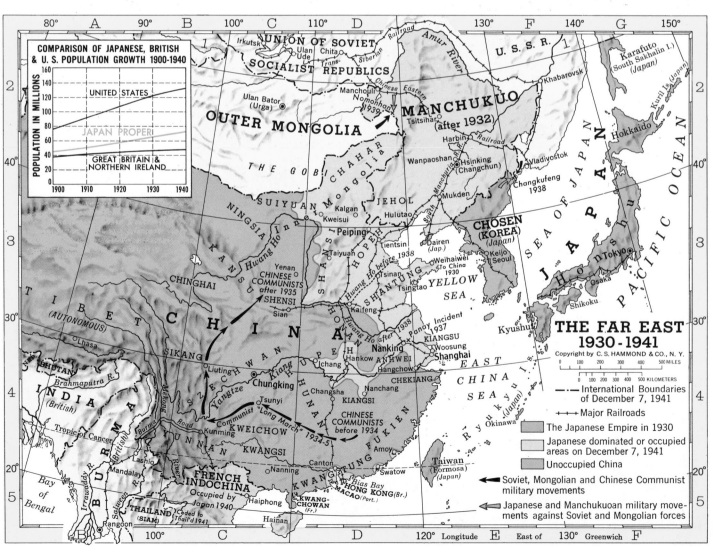

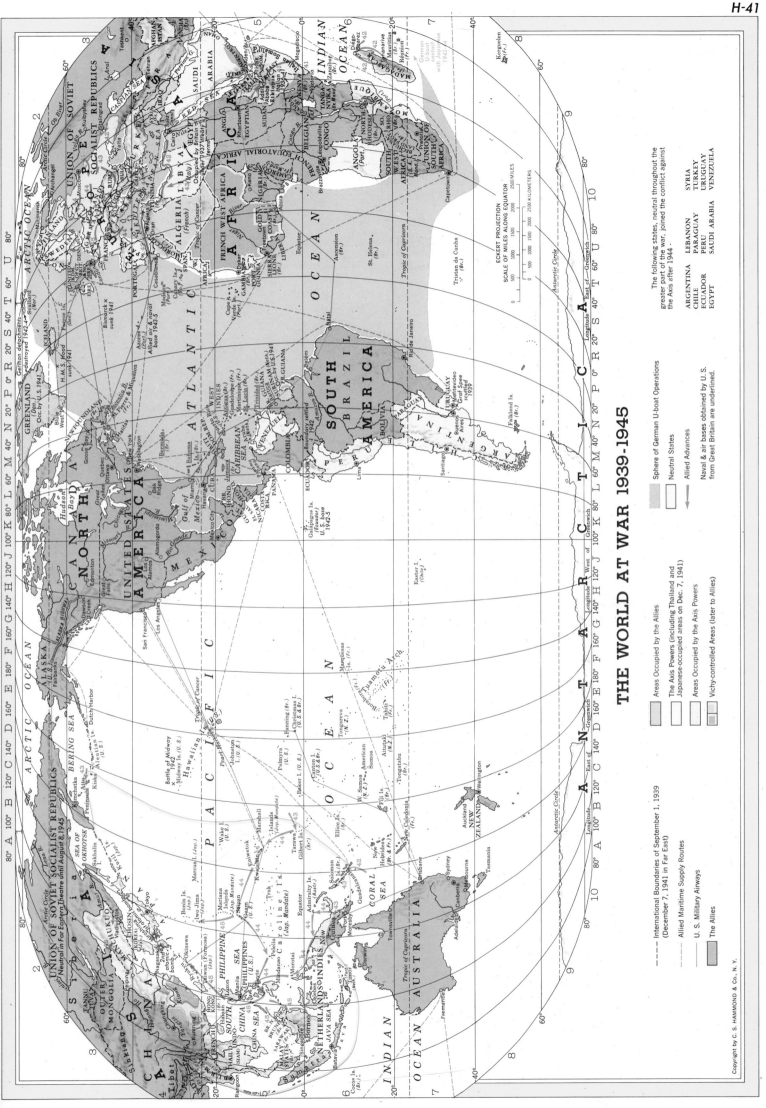

THE WORLD AT WAR 1939-1945

The following states, neutral throughout the greater part of the war, joined the conflict against the Axis after 1944.

ARGENTINA	LEBANON	SYRIA
CHILE	PARAGUAY	TURKEY
ECUADOR	PERU	URUGUAY
EGYPT	SAUDI ARABIA	VENEZUELA

Areas Occupied by the Allies

The Axis Powers (including Thailand and Japanese-occupied areas on Dec. 7, 1941)

Areas Occupied by the Axis Powers

Vichy-controlled Areas (later to Allies)

Sphere of German U-boat Operations

Neutral States

Allied Advances

Naval & air bases obtained by U. S. from Great Britain are underlined.

International Boundaries of September 1, 1939 (December 7, 1941 in Far East)

Allied Maritime Supply Routes

U. S. Military Airways

The Allies

ECKERT PROJECTION
SCALE OF MILES ALONG EQUATOR

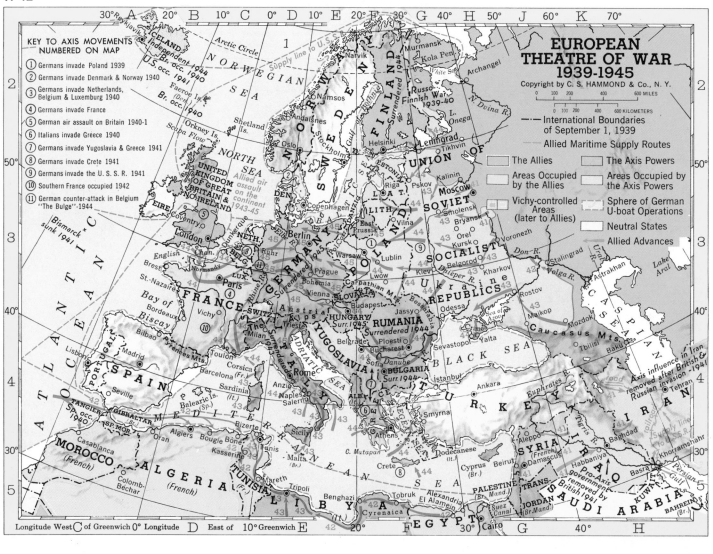

① Germans invade Poland 1939
② Germans invade Denmark & Norway 1940
③ Germans invade Netherlands, Belgium & Luxemburg 1940
④ Germans invade France
⑤ German air assault on Britain 1940-1
⑥ Italians invade Greece 1940
⑦ Germans invade Yugoslavia & Greece 1941
⑧ Germans invade Crete 1941
⑨ Germans invade the U.S.S.R. 1941
⑩ Southern France occupied 1942
⑪ German counter-attack in Belgium "The Bulge"-1944

EUROPEAN THEATRE OF WAR 1939-1945

Copyright by C. S. Hammond & Co., N.Y.

0 100 200	400	600 MILES
0 100 200	400	600 KILOMETERS

— · — International Boundaries of September 1, 1939
——— Allied Maritime Supply Routes

The Allies — The Axis Powers
Areas Occupied by the Allies — Areas Occupied by the Axis Powers
Vichy-controlled Areas (later to Allies) — Sphere of German U-boat Operations
Neutral States
← Allied Advances

FAR EASTERN THEATRE OF WAR 1941-1945

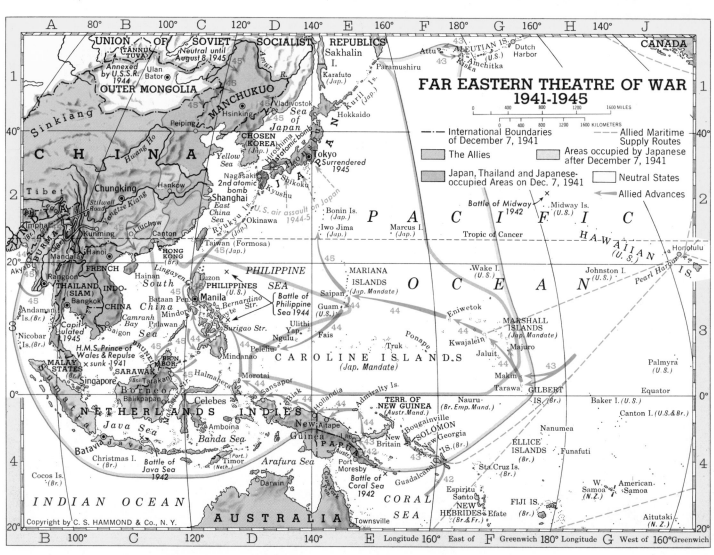

0 400	800	1600 MILES
0 400	800	1600 KILOMETERS

— · — International Boundaries of December 7, 1941
——— Allied Maritime Supply Routes

The Allies — Areas occupied by Japanese after December 7, 1941
Japan, Thailand and Japanese-occupied Areas on Dec. 7, 1941 — Neutral States
← Allied Advances

Copyright by C. S. Hammond & Co., N.Y.

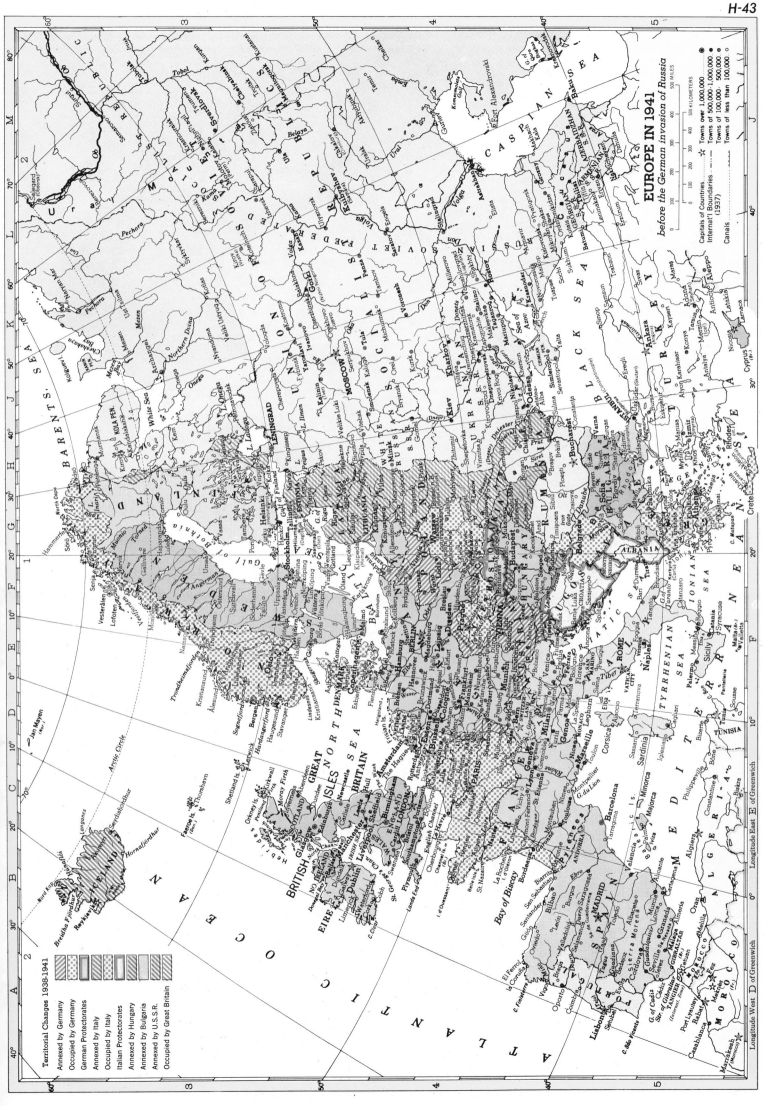

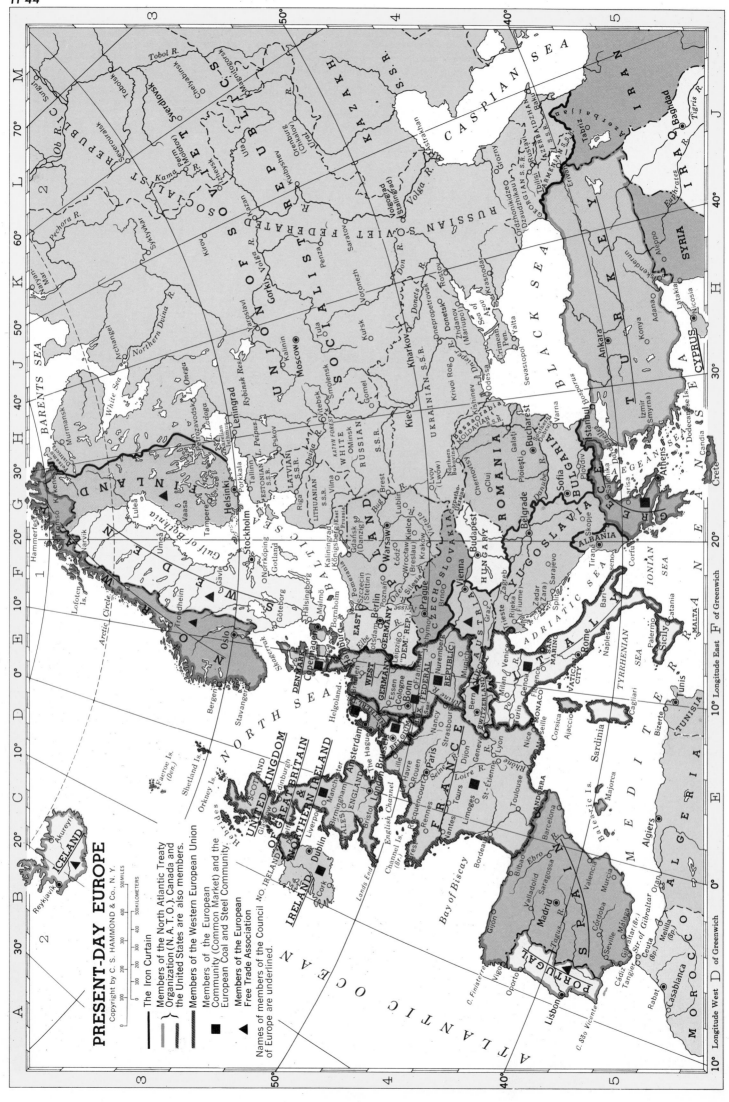

PRESENT-DAY EUROPE

Copyright by C. S. HAMMOND & Co., N.Y.

— The Iron Curtain

〰 Members of the North Atlantic Treaty Organization (N.A.T.O.). Canada and the United States are also members.

▨ Members of the Western European Union

■ Members of the European Community (Common Market) and the European Coal and Steel Community.

▲ Members of the European Free Trade Association

NO. IRELAND Names of members of the Council of Europe are underlined.

0 100 200 300 400 500 MILES

0 100 200 300 400 500 KILOMETERS

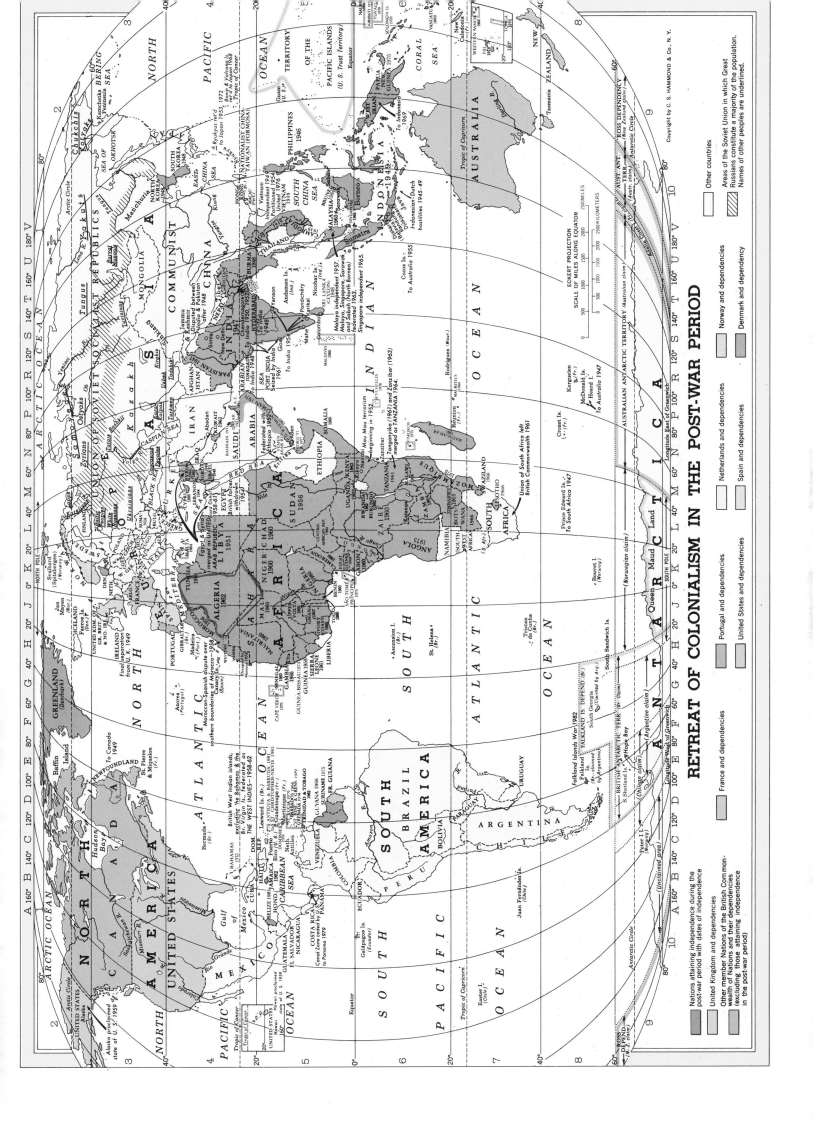

RETREAT OF COLONIALISM IN THE POST-WAR PERIOD

Copyright by C. S. HAMMOND & Co., N. Y.

Legend:

- Nations attaining independence during the post-war period with dates of independence
- United Kingdom and dependencies
- Other member Nations of the British Commonwealth of Nations and their dependencies (excluding those attaining independence in the post-war period)
- France and dependencies
- Portugal and dependencies
- United States and dependencies
- Norway and dependencies
- Denmark and dependency
- Netherlands and dependencies
- Spain and dependencies
- Other countries
- Areas of the Soviet Union in which Great Russians constitute a majority of the population. Names of other peoples are underlined.

ECKERT PROJECTION
SCALE OF MILES ALONG EQUATOR
0 500 1000 1500 2000 2500 MILES
0 500 1000 1500 2000 2500 KILOMETERS

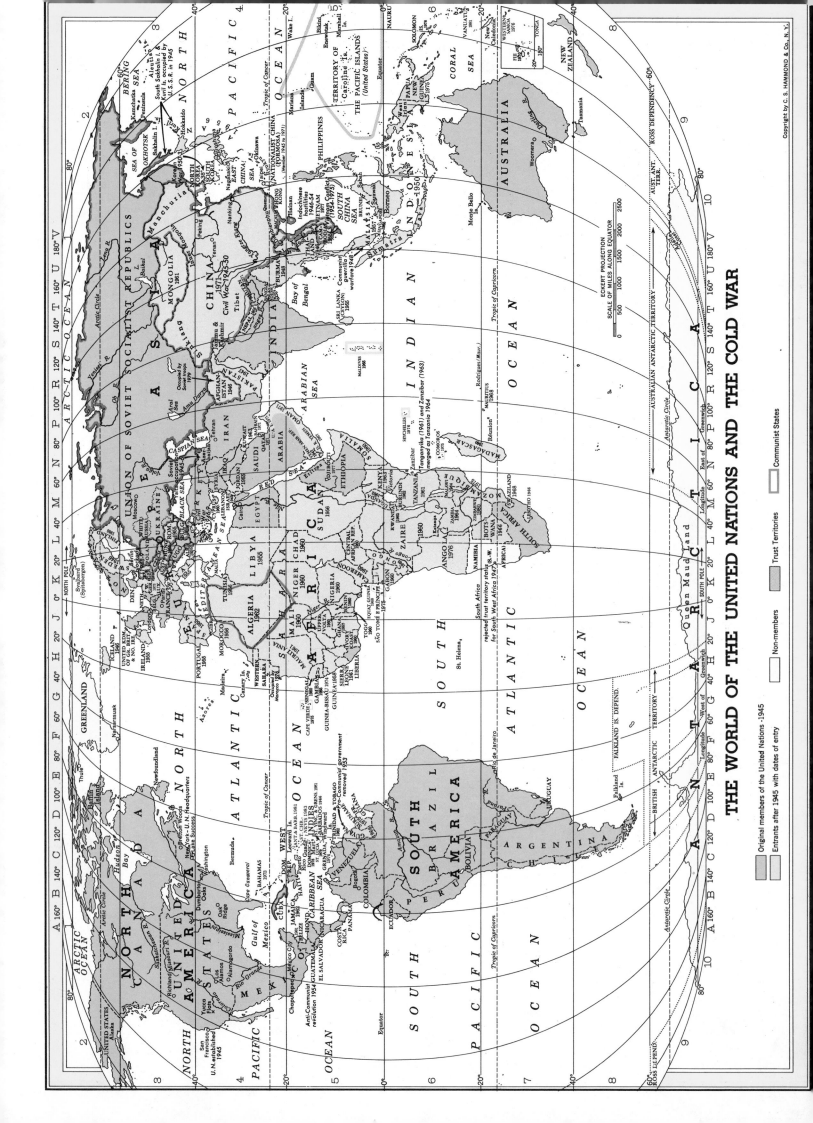

THE WORLD OF THE UNITED NATIONS AND THE COLD WAR

Copyright by C. S. Hammond & Co., N. Y.

ECKERT PROJECTION
SCALE OF MILES ALONG EQUATOR
0   500   1000   1500   2000   2500

Original members of the United Nations -1945

Entrants after 1945 with dates of entry

Non-members

Trust Territories

Communist States

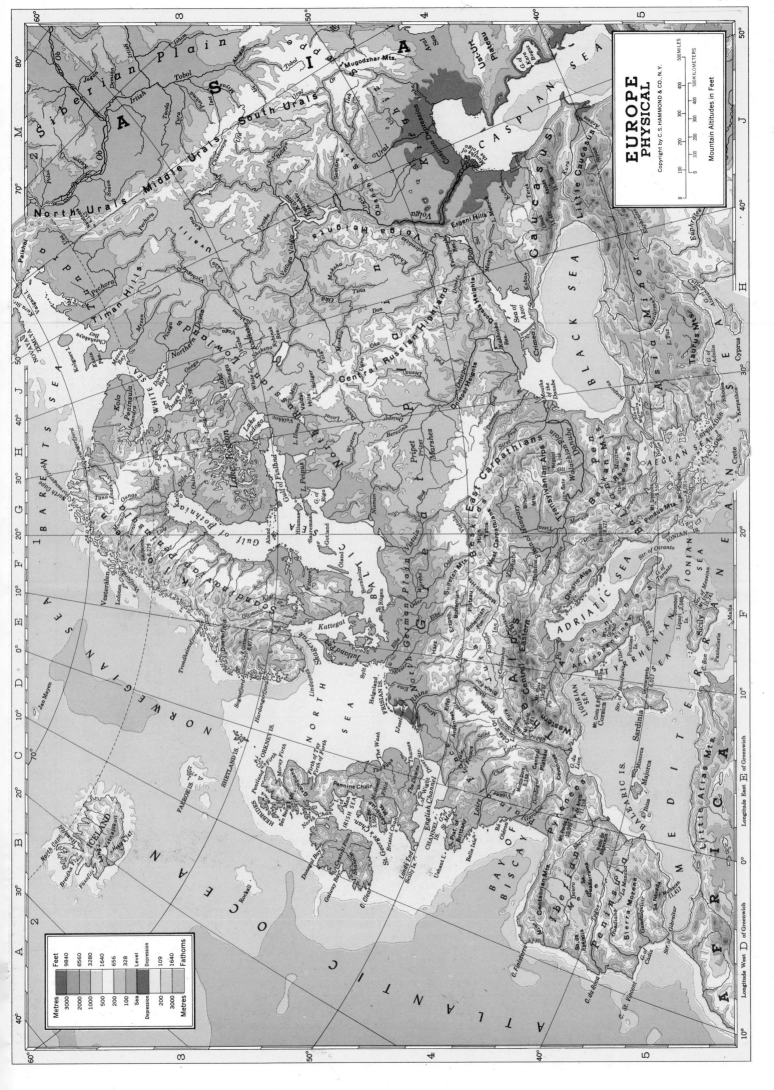

EUROPE
PHYSICAL

Copyright by C. S. HAMMOND & CO., N.Y.

Mountain Altitudes in Feet

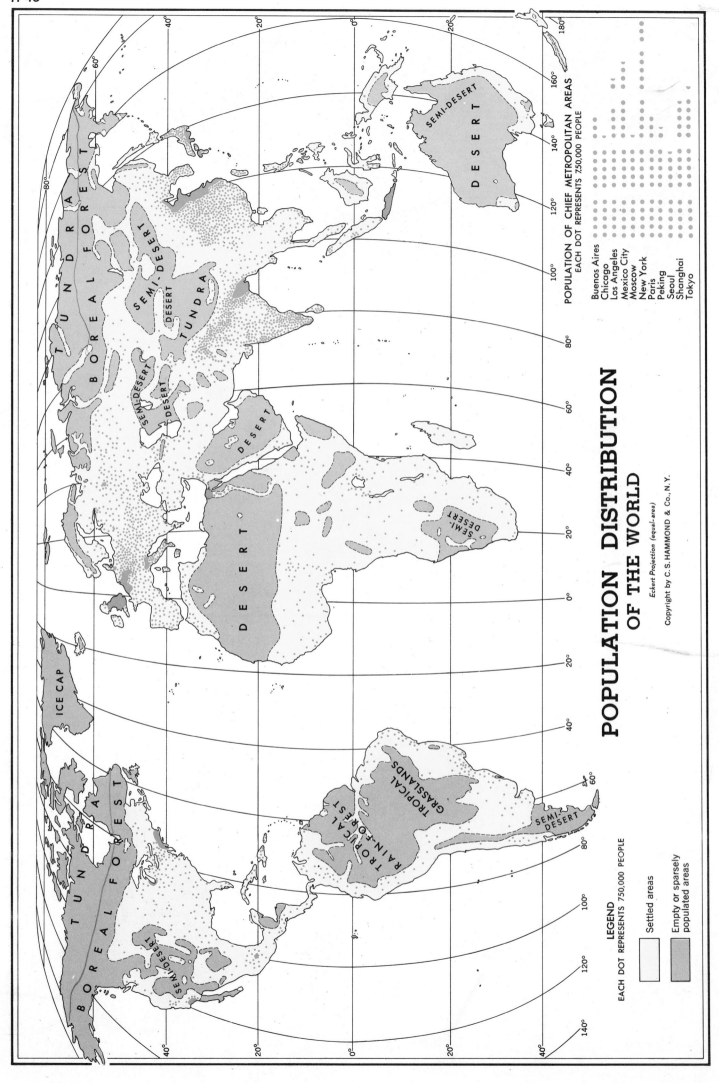

POPULATION DISTRIBUTION OF THE WORLD

Eckert Projection (equal-area)

Copyright by C. S. HAMMOND & Co., N.Y.

POPULATION OF CHIEF METROPOLITAN AREAS
EACH DOT REPRESENTS 750,000 PEOPLE

Buenos Aires
Chicago
Los Angeles
Mexico City
Moscow
New York
Paris
Peking
Seoul
Shanghai
Tokyo

LEGEND
EACH DOT REPRESENTS 750,000 PEOPLE

Settled areas

Empty or sparsely populated areas

INDEX

	Index Ref.	Plate No.

Abadan M-4 H45
Abbasids, Caliphate
  of the C-2 H14
Abo J-6 H34
Abyssinia (Ethiopia)
  (left) F-6 H35
Acadia M-9 H22
Acarnania
  (bottom).......B-2 H 4
Achaia (bottom).B,C-2 H 4
Achaia, Princ. of..F-5 H15
Acre (bottom inset) H13
Acropolis (bottom)A-3 H 4
Actium (bottom)..A-3 H 4
Adalia (bottom)...E-2 H33
Adana (bottom)...E-2 H33
Aden (right).......D-5 H35
Admiralty Is.
  (bottom).......E-4 H42
Adowa (left).......F-5 H35
Adrianople (top)..D-1 H33
Aegean Sea .... H 4
Aegina (bottom)...C-3 H 4
Aeolis (bottom)...E-2 H 4
Aetolia (bottom)..B-2 H 4
Afghanistan (right) E-4 H35
Africa (Roman
  prov.) ....K-7 H 5
Agadir (left).......A-3 H35
Agincourt W-20 H18
Aiguesmortes
  (bottom).......A-2 H13
Aigun F-7 H34
Aisne River.......L-3 H37
Aix-la-Chapelle ..E-2 H 9
Ajanta D-2 H14
Akyab (bottom)...B-3 H42
Alamanni ....D-3 H 7
Alans ....L-3,A-4 H 7
Alaska Highway..H-2 H41
Albania G-4 H36
Albi D-6 H18
Alcazar (El Ksar
  el Kebir) A-7 H20
Alemania ....E-3 H 9
Aleutian Is.
  (bottom).......G-1 H42
Alexander's Empire H 5
Alexandretta
  (bottom).......E-2 H33
Alexandria (top)..B-4 H 4
Algeciras D-5 H36
Algeria (left).......C-4 H35
Algiers (left).......C-3 H35
Almería (top).......B-4 H40
Almohades,
  Dominions of the.D-5 H15
Almoravids, Domin-
  ions of the(top)..B-3 H13
Alsace & Lorraine..B-3 H31
Amalfi (top).......E-2 H13
Amberg (left).......E-4 H26
Amiens K-5 H37
Amoy (bottom)...D-4 H40
Amur District.......F-6 H34
Anatolia E-2 H33
Anbar (bottom)...G-3 H11
Andorra C-5 H23
Andrussof D-3 H24
Angevin Empire H18
Angkor F-3 H14
Angles ....D-2 H 7
Angora (Ankara)..E-1 H33
Anjou O-16 H18
Antioch
  (bottom inset).... H13
Antonine Wall B-2 H10
Anzio (bottom)....E-3 H42
Aquae Solis (Bath).C-4 H10
Aquileia ....D-2 H 6
Aquitaine ....D-3 H 9
Arabia C-2 H14
Arbela ....D-2 H 5
Arcadia (bottom)..C-3 H 4
Arelate ....L-4 H 9
Argentina (right).. H29
Argonne Forest ...L-5 H37
Argos (bottom) ....C-3 H 4
Armenia F-1 H33
Arras K-4 H37
Artois Q-14 H18
Aryans ....Map A H 2
Asad (top).......G-4 H11
Ascalon (bottom inset) H13
Ashdod (top).......A-4 H 4
Asia (Roman
  prov.) ....M-7 H 5
Asia Minor F-3 H11
Asir (right).......D-5 H35
Asoka's Empire...D-2 H14
Aspromonte F-5 H30
Assab (left).......G-5 H35
Assassins
  (bottom inset).... H13
Assyria (top).......F-2 H 3
Astrakhan,
  Khanate of F-3 H34
Asturias, Kdm. of
  Galicia & ....B-4 H 9
Athens (bottom)...A-3 H 4
Athens, Duchy of..F-5 H15
Attica (bottom)....C-3 H 4
Attu (bottom).......F-1 H42
Augsburg E-4 H15
Ausculum ....E-4 H 6
Austerlitz J-4 H27
Austrasia ....E-2 H 9
Austria F-6 H38
Austria-Hungary ..F-4 H36
Austrian
  Netherlands ...G-3 H22
Auvergne Q-17 H18
Avar Kingdom ....E-3 H 8
Avignon C-5 H21
Axis Powers H41
Axum F-5 H11
Axumite
  Kingdom ....Map C H 2

Ayacucho (right)... H29
Ayyubids, Sult. of
  the (bottom).......H-4 H13
Azd (top).......G-5 H11
Azerbaijan
  (bottom).......K-3 H13
Azores N-4 H41
Azov F-1 H33
Aztec Empire ..Map D H 2
Babylon (bottom)..D-2 H 3
Babylonian Empire.
Bactria (bottom)..F-2 H 3
Badajoz (left).......B-4 H40
Badr (Bedr) (top).F-4 H11
Baden (top).......C-3 H31
Baghdad ....M-6 H 9
Bagirmi (left).......D-5 H35
Bagtiginids H-5 H15
Bahia (Salvador)
  (left) H29
Bahrain (region)
  (bottom).......G-4 H11
Bakr (top).......A-4 H11
Balaklava A-5 H34
Balearic Is.
  (bottom).......A-3 H13
Balkh (bottom)....J-3 H11
Banat L-4 H22
Bandung R-6 H45
Bangkok (top).......R-5 H45
Bar H-8 H24
Bar, Duchy of.......R-15 H18
Barbados G-5 H45
Barbary States K-3 H34
Barca (bottom)....E-3 H11
Barcelona C-3 H12
Bardo (bottom)....B-2 H33
Bari (top).......F-2 H13
Barotseland (left).E-8 H35
Basel (left).......D-4 H26
Basques ....B-3 H 8
Basra D-3 H11
Bastarnae ....M-6 H 5
Bastille (bottom)..D-3 H25
Bataan Pen.
  (bottom).......C-3 H42
Batavia (right).......G-6 H35
Batavian Rep.
  (left) D-3 H26
Batum A-6 H34
Bavaria, Kdm. of
  (top) C-3 H31
Bavarians ....D-3 H 8
Belém (Para) H29
Belgium (top).......B-2 H31
Belgorod (top).......G-3 H42
Belgrade (top).......C-1 H33
Belize (bottom).... H29
Belleau Wood K-5 H37
Benadir (left).......G-6 H35
Benevento,
  Duchy of ....G-4 H 9
Beneventum ....E-4 H 6
Benghazi (top).......E-4 H42
Berbers ....C-4 H 8
Berchtesgaden
  (top) D-3 H40
Beresina River L-3 H27
Berlin F-3 H36
Bermuda E-3 H19
Bernicia R-14 H10
Berry P-16 H18
Berwick B-2 H20
Bessarabia D-1 H33
Bethlehem (top)...D-4 H 4
Biak (bottom).......D-4 H42
Bias Bay(bottom).D-4 H40
Bikini U-5 H46
Bilbao (top).......B-3 H40
Birmingham G-5 H32
Bithynia ....N-6 H 5
Bizerte (top).......B-2 H42
Björkö G-2 H36
Blenheim J-4 H22
Blois J-10 H18
Bluie West 1.......M-2 H41
Bodh Gaya E-2 H14
Boeotia (bottom)..C-2 H 4
Bogotá F-5 H46
Bohemia E-4 H15
Bohemia-Moravia
  (Prot.)(top) D-2 H40
Bokhara B-7 H34
Bolivia (right).......... H29
Bona (Bone).......C-3 H11
Bonn B-3 H26
Bornu (left).......D-5 H35
Borobudur F-4 H14
Borodino N-2 H27
Bosnia F-4 H36
Boulogne (right)...F-3 H27
Bourbon
  Dominions H20,H22
Boyacá (right).......... H29
Brandenburg E-3 H21
Brazil H29
Breitenfeld E-3 H21
Brest Litovsk G-3 H36
Bretigny Q-15 H18
Bretton Woods F-3 H46
Brittany B-9 H18
Brundisium ....F-4 H 6
Brunswick (top)...C-2 H31
Brussels E-3 H43
Bucharest G-4 H38
Buda (top).......C-1 H33
Budapest G-4 H38
Buenos Aires H29
Bukovina (bottom).D-1 H33
Bulawayo (left).......F-9 H35
Bulgaria (bottom).E-2 H15
Bulgarian Emp.
  (bottom).......E-2 H11
Bulge, Battle
  of the (top).......D-2 H43
Burgos (top).......B-3 H40
Burgundians ....F-2,D-3 H 7
Burgundy X-22 H18

Burgundy, Upper .M-4 H 9
Burma E-2 H14
Burma Road
  (bottom).......B-4 H40
Bursa (Brusa) D-1 H33
Byzantine Emp. H14
Byzantium ....M-6 H 5
Cádiz J-3 H19
Caesarea
  (bottom inset) .. H13
Cairo S-4 H41
Cairo, Califate
  of (top) C-4 H11
Calais P-14 H18
Calcutta E-2 H14
Caledonia ....C-1 H 9
Cambodia, Emp.of.F-3 H14
Cambrai C-3 H20
Campo Formio
  (left) E-4 H26
Canal Zone (right). H29
Candia (Crete).......H-7 H21
Cannae ....F-4 H 6
Canterbury
  (Cantwarabyrig).K-8 H10
Canton (bottom)...D-4 H40
Caporetto (right)..E-1 H30
Cappadocia ....N-7 H 5
Caprivi Zipfel
  (left) E-8 H35
Capua (top).......E-2 H13
Carabobo (right)... H29
Caracas H29
Carchemish (top)..E-1 H 4
Carlsbad E-3 H28
Caroline Is.
  (bottom).......E-3 H42
Carolingian
  Kingdom .... H 9
Carpatho-Ukraine
  (top) E-3 H40
Cartagena
  (Colombia) H29
Cartagena (Spain)D-5 H36
Carthage ....Map B H 2
Casablanca (top)..C-4 H42
Castelfidardo
  (right) F-3 H30
Castile C-4 H15
Catalan Counties
  (top) C-2 H13
Catalonia (top)....C-3 H40
Catalonian Fields ..C-3 H 7
Cawnpore D-2 H14
Celts ....Map B H 2
Central American
  Confederation (right) H29
Cerignola F-5 H20
Ceuta (bottom)....B-3 H11
Ceylon P-5 H45
Chaeronea
  (bottom).......C-2 H 4
Chaghatai,
  Khanate of D-1 H14
Chalcidice
  (bottom).......C-1 H 4
Chalcis (bottom)...C-2 H 4
Châlons ....C-3 H 8
Champa F-3 H14
Champagne K-9 H18
Changkufeng
  (top) F-2 H40
Chapultepec D-5 H46
Château-Cambrésis.C-3 H20
Château-Thierry ..K-5 H37
Chaumont C-4 H28
Chemin des Dames.K-5 H37
Chengtu F-2 H14
Cherchel (bottom).C-3 H11
Chile H29
China....Maps A,B,C & D H14
China F-2 H14
Chinese Eastern R.R.
  (bottom).......D-2 H40
Chinese Rep. (right)G-3 H35
Chioggia (left).......E-2 H30
Chios (bottom)....D-2 H 4
Chosen (right).......H-3 H35
Chungking
  (bottom).......C-4 H40
"Cibola" B-3 H19
Cid, Dom. of the
  (bottom).......B-3 H13
Cilicia (bottom)...G-2 H 3
Circassians K-5 H28
Cisalpine Rep.(Italian
  Rep.) (left).......D-4 H26
Ciudad de los Reyes
  (Lima) (left) H29
Clermont (top).......C-1 H43
Cleve (right).......B-2 H26
Cnossus (bottom).B-3 H 4
Cocos Is. P-6 H45
Coimbra C-4 H15
Colchis ....O-6 H 5
Cologne (right).......B-3 H26
Colombia (right).... H29
Communist China.P-4 H46
Compiegne K-5 H37
Confederation of the
  Rhine H27
Constance E-1 H33
Constantinople,
  (top) F-4 H15
Constantinople,
Coral Sea (bottom)E-4 H42
Cordova,
  Caliphate of ....C-5 H 9
Corfu (Kerkyra)....F-5 H38
Corinth
  (bottom).......C-3 H 4
Corsica (bottom)..B-1 H 9
Costa Rica (right). H29
Courland, Duchy of.G-2 H23
Covadonga
  (bottom).......B-2 H11
Coventry (top).......C-2 H28
Cracow, Rep. of..G-3 H28
Crécy Q-14 H18
Cremona D-4 H15

Crete (bottom)....B-3 H 4
Crete (top).......F-4 H42
Crimea A-5 H34
Crimea, Khanate
  of the J-4 H20
Croatia (top).......F-2 H13
Crusades H13
Ctesiphon
  (Madain) (top)..G-3 H11
Cuba (right).......... H29
Cumae ....D-4 H 6
Cumans F-4 H15
Custozza (right)...D-2 H30
Cuzco H29
Cyclades (bottom).D-3 H 4
Cyprus, Kdm. of
  (bottom).......G-3 H13
Cyrenaica (left)....E-3 H35
Cyzicus (bottom)..E-1 H 4
Czechoslovakia F-3 H38
Dacia ....M-6 H 5
Dagestan
  (Daghestan) A-6 H34
Dakar P-5 H41
Dalmatia ....L-6 H 5
Damascus (top)...E-3 H 4
Damascus
  (bottom).......F-3 H11
Damascus, Emir. of
  (bottom inset) .. H13
Damietta
  (bottom).......G-4 H13
Danelaw, The S-15 H10
Danes ....F-1 H 9
Danishmand
  Emirate (top)...K-3 H13
Danzig J-3 H43
Danzig, Rep. of....K-1 H27
Dara (Daras) ....G-4 H 8
Dardanelles G-5 H36
Darfur (left).......E-5 H35
Dauphiné X-23 H18
Decelea (bottom)..C-2 H 4
Delagoa Bay (left).F-9 H35
Delhi D-2 H14
Delos (bottom)....D-3 H 4
Delphi (bottom)...C-2 H 4
Denmark E-3 H15
Denmark & Norway,
  Kdm. of D-2 H20
Derbent (bottom)..G-2 H11
Dettingen (right)..E-3 H26
Dienbienphu R-4 H46
Djakarta R-6 H45
Dobrudja
  (bottom).......D-1 H33
Dodecanese
  (bottom).......D-3 H 4
Dominican Rep.
  (right) H29
Domremy X-21 H18
Don Cossacks H-3 H34
Dongola, Kdm. of..F-5 H11
Doris (bottom).......E-3 H 4
Dorylaeum (top)...H-3 H13
Drepanum ....D-6 H 6
Dresden H-3 H27
Dumbarton Oaks ..E-4 H46
Dunkerque (top)...D-2 H42
Durazzo F-4 H36
Durban (left).......F-9 H35
Dutch East Indies
  (right) G-6 H35
Dvin (top).......G-2 H11
Dzungaria (right)..F-3 H35
East Africa Prot.
  (left) F-6 H35
East Anglia P-11 H10
East Frankish Kdm.N-2 H 9
East Friesland D-3 H23
East Goths ....J-3,F-3 H 7
East Prussia (top).E-2 H40
East Germany
  ("Dem." Rep.)...F-3 H44
Eastern Roman
  Empire .... H 7, H 8
Eastern Rumelia
  (bottom).......D-1 H33
Ecbatana (bottom)D-2 H 3
Ecuador (right).... H29
Edessa, County of
  (bottom inset) ..A-2 H13
Edinburgh B-2 H20
Egypt (Ancient)....C-4 H 3
Eire C-3 H43
El Alamein (top)...F-4 H42
Elam (top).......D-2 H 5
Elba E-5 H28
Elea ....E-4 H 6
Elis (bottom).......B-3 H 4
Empire, The D-3 H21
Eniwetok T-5 H46
Ephesus (top).......B-2 H 5
Epirus (bottom)....B-2 H 4
Epirus,
  Despotate of F-4 H15
Erfurt (top).......C-2 H31
Eritrea (left).......F-5 H35
Eskishehr (left)....E-2 H33
Essen (bottom)....B-2 H31
Essex (East
  Saxonia) O-12 H10
Estonia G-3 H38
Ethiopia ....Map D H 2
Etruria ....C-3 H 6
Etruria, Kdm. of
  (left) E-5 H26
Euboea (bottom)..C-2 H 4
Eupen M-4 H37
Eylau, Preussisch-.K-3 H27
Fairbanks G-2 H41
Falkland Is. (right).F-5 H35
Fashoda (left).......F-5 H35
Fatimite
  Caliphate (top)..J-4 H13
Ferrara, Duchy of
  (left) D-2 H30

Fez (left).......B-3 H35
Fez and Morocco..B-7 H20
Fezzan (left).......D-4 H35
Finland (top).......F-2 H42
Fiume F-4 H38
Flanders Q-14 H18
Fleurus (left).......C-3 H26
Flodden B-2 H20
Florence, Rep. of
  (left) D-3 H30
Fontainebleau F-4 H27
Fontenoy(Belgium)G-3 H22
Fontenoy (France).J-1 H 9
Formosa G-2 H14
Fort Duquesne
  (Ft. Pitt) K-12 H22
France H18
Franche Comté D-4 H20
Franconia D-4 H15
Frank Kingdoms ..C-3 H 8
Frankfurt
  (Frankfort) D-3 H28
Frankish Kingdom..D-3 H 9
French Empire
  (Napoleonic) H27
Friedland K-3 H27
Frisians ....C-2 H 8
Füssen E-4 H23
Fustat (bottom)....F-3 H11
Gaeta (right).......E-3 H30
Galápagos Is. K-6 H41
Galatia ....N-7 H 5
Galicia G-8 H24
Galilee (top).......D-3 H 4
Gallia Cisalpina ....B-2 H 6
Gambela (left).......F-6 H35
Gascony B-6 H18
Gastein (top).......D-3 H31
Gaugamela ....E-2 H 5
Gaul ....K-6 H 5
Gaza (top).......D-3 H 4
Gedrosia (bottom).F-3 H 3
Gela ....E-6 H 6
General-
  Gouvernement ..G-3 H43
Geneva E-4 H38
Genoa, Rep. of
  (left) C-2 H30
Georgia (Russia)..A-6 H34
Georgia, Kdm. of
  (bottom).......J-2 H13
Gepids ....G-3 H 7
German Confedera-
  tion (top).......... H31
German East Africa
  (bottom).......F-7 H 35
German Empire
  (top) H36
German Southwest
  Africa (left).......D-9 H35
Germania ....L-5 H 5
Ghana,
  Kdm. of ....Map C H 2
Ghassanid Kingdom.F-4 H 8
Ghent (top).......A-2 H31
Gibraltar F-6 H22
Gnesen E-3 H15
Godesberg (top)...C-2 H40
Golden Horde,
  Khanate of the..C-1 H14
Goose Bay L-3 H41
Goshen (top).......B-4 H 4
Goths ....F-2,J-3,B-4 H 7
Granada B-4 H20
Great Britain & Ire-
  land, Kdm. of ...E-3 H22
Greece G-5 H38
Greece, Ancient .... H 4
Greenland M-2 H41
Grossjägermdorf ..G-3 H23
Guadalajara (left). H29
Guadalcanal
  (bottom).......E-4 H42
Guadalete
  (bottom).......B-3 H11
Guatemala H29
Guinea J-5 H45
Gupta Empire....Map C H 2
Gurganj H-2 H11
Guthrum,
  Kdm. of T-16 H10
Guyenne J-11 H18
Habbaniya (top)...H-4 H42
Habsburg Dominions H23
Hadhramaut H-5 H11
Hadrian's Wall C-2 H10
Hadrianopolis
  (Adrianople) E-2 H11
Hafsids (bottom)..B-3 H13
Hague, The B-3 H36
Haiti (right).......... H29
Halicarnassus
  (bottom).......E-3 H 4
Hamburg D-2 H36
Hammadites (top).C-3 H13
Han Empire F-2 H14
Hangchow F-2 H14
Hankow (bottom)..D-3 H40
Hanover (top).......C-2 H31
Hanseatic League... H17
Harappa D-1 H14
Harbin (right).......H-3 H35
Harran (bottom)...B-3 H11
Hasa (right).......D-4 H35
Hastenbeck (right).E-1 H26
Hastings C-2 H18
Hatay (right).......F-2 H40
Hattin (Hittin)
  (bottom inset) .. H13
Hattushash B-1 H14
Havana (La Habana) H29
Hawaiian Is. F-4 H41
Hawazin (top).......G-4 H11
Hazaraspids H-5 H15
Hebron (top).......H 4
Hejaz (right).......C-4 H35
Helgoland E-3 H36

Heliopolis (on)
  (top) ....B-4 H 4
Hellas (bottom)..... H 4
Helvetian Rep.
  (left) D-4 H26
Heraclea ....F-4 H 6
Herat (top).......J-3 H11
Herculaneum ....E-4 H 6
Hesse (top).......C-2 H31
Himera ....D-6 H 6
Himyaritic
  Kdm. ....Map C H 2
Hippo
  (Hippo Regius) ..C-4 H 8
Hira (top).......G-3 H11
Hiroshima(bottom) D-2 H42
Hispania (Spain)..J-6 H 5
Hispaniola
  (Española) (left). H29
Hittite
  Civilization .. Map A H 2
Hiung-Nu ....Map B H 2
Höchstädt (right).F-5 H26
Hohenlinden (left).E-4 H26
Hohenzollern C-3 H31
Holstein (top).......C-2 H31
Holy Roman
  Empire D-4 H15
Homs (top).......F-3 H11
Honduras (right)... H29
Hong Kong F-2 H14
Hope Bay G-9 H45
Hotel de Ville
  (bottom).......D-2 H25
Hubertusburg E-3 H23
Hué (right).......G-5 H35
Hungary F-3 H15
Hungary, Kdm. of.E-3 H31
Huns ....H 7, H14
Hydaspes River ...H 5
Iceland (left).......B-1 H42
Iconium, Sult. of..H-3 H13
Ilium (Troy)
  (bottom).......E-2 H 4
Illyrian Provinces..H-4 H27
Illyricum ....F-7 H 7
Imphal (bottom)...B-2 H42
Inca Empire ... Map D H 2
India D,E-4 H14
Indian Empire
  (right) E-4 H35
Indonesia R-6 H45
Indus Valley
  Civilization D-2 H14
Iona F-5 H10
Ionia (bottom).......E-2 H 4
Ionian Islands F-6 H28
Ipsus ....N-5 H 5
Ireland J-3 H45
Irish Free State C-3 H38
Isfahan (Ispahan).C-2 H14
Islam H11
Israel, Kdm. of
  (top) ....D-4 H 4
Israel, Rep. of L-4 H45
Issus ....C-2 H 5
Istakhr (top).......D-4 H11
Italian East Africa.T-5 H41
Italian Republic
  (1803) (left).......D-4 H26
Itil B-3 H34
Iviza (bottom).......C-3 H11
Ivry C-4 H20
Iwo Jima (bottom).E-2 H42
Jacobins, les
  (bottom).......C-1 H25
Jankau E-4 H21
Japan G-2 H14
Jassy H-7 H34
Java Sea (bottom).C-4 H42
Jena D-3 H27
Jerba K-3 H19
Jericho (top).......D-4 H 4
Jerusalem (top)....B-3 H 4
Jerusalem, Kdm. of
  (bottom inset) .. H13
Jordan L-4 H45
Jubaland (left).......G-6 H35
Judah, Kdm. of
  (top) ....D-4 H 4
Jülich (right).......B-3 H26
Jutes ....D-1 H 7
Kabul J-3 H11
Kaifeng (bottom)..D-3 H40
Kairwan (top).......D-3 H13
Kalisch J-3 H27
Kalmar F-2 H20
Kama Bulgaria H-3 H15
Kamerun (left).......D-6 H35
Kandahar J-3 H11
Kapilavastu E-2 H14
Karafuto (right).......J-3 H35
Karakorum F-1 H14
Karbala (Kerbela)
  (top) G-3 H11
Karkar (top).......E-2 H 4
Kars E-2 H34
Kashmir, Jammu &.P-4 H46
Kasserine (top).......D-4 H42
Katanga (left).......E-8 H35
Katyn Forest G-3 H44
Kazan, Khanate of.F-2 H34
Kent (Cantia) P-12 H10
Kerch (bottom).......E-1 H34
Khanbalik F-1 H14
Kharkov (right).......G-3 H42
Khartoum
  (bottom).......E-4 H33
Khazars, Emp.
  of the B-3 H34
Khelat (bottom)...J-3 H13
Khiva B-7 H34
Khmer Empire F-3 H14
Khorasan (top).......H-3 H11
Khwarizm
  (bottom).......H-2 H11
Khyber Pass D-2 H14
Kiaochow (right)..G-4 H35
Kiel Canal E-3 H36

	Index Ref.	Plate No.
Kiev	A-2	H34
Kimberley (left)	E-9	H35
Kinda (top)	G-4	H11
Kiska (bottom)	F-1	H42
Königgrätz (top)	D-2	H31
Königsberg	F-3	H21
Korea	G-2	H14
Kossovo (top)	D-1	H33
Kronstadt	G-3	H36
Kuchuk-Kainarji	J-7	H34
Kufa	G-3	H11
Kunersdorf	F-3	H23
Kunming (bottom)	C-4	H40
Kurdistan (bottom)	J-3	H13
Kursk (top)	G-3	H42
Kushan States	Map C	H 2
Kut al Imara (bottom)	F-2	H33
Kwajalein (right)	F-3	H42
Kwangchowwan (right)	G-4	H40
La Plata, Río de		H29
La Rochelle	B-4	H21
Lado (left)	F-6	H35
Ladysmith (left)	F-9	H35
Lake Success	F-3	H46
Lakhmid Kdm. (top)	G-3	H11
Langensalza (top)	C-2	H31
Languedoc	K-12	H18
Laos	R-5	H45
Lashio (bottom)	B-4	H40
Latin Empire (bottom)	E-3	H13
		H 6
Latium	D-4	H 6
Latvia	G-3	H38
Lausanne	E-4	H38
Lebanon	L-4	H45
Ledo (bottom)	B-2	H42
Leipzig	H-3	H27
Lemberg	F-3	H36
Leningrad (top)	G-2	H42
Leoben	F-4	H26
Leon	C-4	H15
Lepanto (top)	D-2	H33
Lesbos (bottom)	E-2	H 4
Lesser Armenia (bottom inset)		H13
Leyte (bottom)	D-3	H42
Libya (left)	D-4	H35
Liechtenstein (left)	E-6	H26
Ligurian Rep. (left)	D-5	H26
Lima		H29
Lindistarne (Holy I.)	J-6	H10
Lingayen Gulf (bottom)	C-3	H42
Lithuania	G-3	H38
Lithuania, Grand Duchy of	H-3	H20
Lithuanians	E-2	H 8
Livonia	C-2	H24
Lobito Bay (left)	D-8	H35
Lodz	C-1	H37
Lombard League		H15
Lombards	E-2	H 7
Lombards, Kdm. of the	D-3	H 8
Lombardy-Venetia	E-4	H28
Londinium (London)	E-4	H10
Loos	K-4	H37
Lorraine, Duchy of	H-4	H22
Lotharingia	K-1	H 9
Louisbourg	M-9	H22
Loyang	F-2	H14
Lübeck	E-3	H21
Lublin	G-3	H20
Lucca, Rep. of (left)	D-3	H30
Lunéville (left)	D-4	H26
Luristan	F-2	H33
Lusitania	J-7	H 5
Lützen	E-3	H21
Luxemburg, Grand Duchy of (top)	B-3	H31
Luzon (top)	D-3	H42
Lydian Kdm. (bottom)	B-2	H 3
Macedonia (bottom)	B-1	H 4
Madagascar	T-6	H41
Madain (Ctesiphon) (top)	G-3	H11
Madjapahit Kdm.	G-4	H14
Madrid	B-5	H20
Mafeking (left)	E-9	H35
Magadha Kdm.	E-2	H14
Magdeburg	E-3	H21
Magenta (right)	C-2	H30
Magnano (left)	E-4	H26
Magnesia (bottom)		H13
Magyars (600 A.D.)	G-2	H 8
Mahedia (top)	C-2	H33
Maine (France)	D-4	H18
Mainz	D-4	H26
Maipú (right)		H29
Malmedy	M-4	H37
Malolos (right)	G-5	H35
Malplaquet	G-4	H22
Malta	E-6	H20
Malta (top)	E-4	H42
Manchester	G-5	H32
Manchukuo (bottom)	E-2	H40
Manila (bottom)	D-3	H42
Mantinea (bottom)	C-3	H 4
Mantua (left)	D-2	H30
Manzikert (top)		H13
Maragha (bottom)	K-3	H13
Marathon (bottom)	C-2	H 4
Marcomanni	L-6	H 5
Marengo (left)	D-5	H26
Mareth (top)	E-4	H42
Mariana Is. (bottom)	E-3	H42
Mark (right)	C-2	H26
Marne River	L-5	H37
Marrakesh	C-5	H15
Marshall Is. (bottom)	F-3	H42
Mataram	Map D	
Matabeleland (left)	E-8	H35
Mauretania	J-7	H 5
Mayan States	Maps C & D	H 2
Mecca (top)	G-4	H11
Mecklenburg	D 2	H31
Median Emp. (bottom)		H 3
Medina (top)	G-4	H11
Megara (bottom)	C-2	H 4
Megiddo (top)	D-3	H 4
Memel (top)	D-2	H40
Memphis (top)	C-4	H 3
Mentana (right)	E-3	H30
Mercia	O-11	H10
Merj Dabik (top)	E-2	H33
Mersen	N-2	H 9
Merv	N-2	H14
Mesopotamia (top)	D-2	H 5
Messana	E-5	H 6
Messenia (bottom)	B-3	H 4
Metz (top)	B-3	H31
Meuse River	L-5	H37
Mexico		H29
Midway Is. (bottom)	G-2	H42
Milan (left)	C-2	H30
Minaean Civilization	Map A	H 2
Minoan Civilization	Map A	H 2
Minorca	G-5	H22
Missolonghi (bottom)	C-2	H33
Moab (top)	D-4	H 4
Modena, Duchy of (left)	D-2	H30
Moesia	M-6	H 5
Mogul Empire	Map D	H 2
Mohacs (top)	C-1	H33
Mohenjo Daro	D-2	H14
Moldavia	D-1	H33
Monaco	D-5	H23
Mongolia	R-3	H46
Mongols	F-1	H14
Mons	K-4	H37
Monte Bello Is.	R-6	H46
Montenegro	F-4	H36
Montevideo		H29
Montferrat	D-5	H20
Moravian Kdm.	N-4	H 9
Morea	L-6	H22
Morocco (left)	B-3	H35
Morotai (bottom)	D-3	H42
Moscow (top)	G-2	H42
Moscow, Principality of	F-2	H34
Mosul	H-5	H15
Mukden (right)	H-3	H35
Munich (top)	D-3	H40
Murmansk (top)	G-1	H42
Muscovy (inset)	E-1	H34
Mutina	C-2	H 6
Mycenae (bottom)	C-3	H 4
Mylae	E-5	H 6
Mysia (top)	B-2	H 5
Nagasaki (bottom)	D-2	H14
Nanchao	E-2	H14
Nanking (bottom)	D-3	H40
Nantes	B-4	H20
Naples, Kdm. of (left)	F-4	H30
Nara	G-2	H14
Narbonne	D-4	H 9
Narvik (top)	E-1	H42
Nassau (top)	C-2	H31
Nationalist China (Formosa)	S-4	H46
Navarino (bottom)	D-2	H33
Navarre	C-4	H15
Naxos (right)	F-3	H13
Nazareth (top)	D-3	H 4
Negroport	G-6	H20
Nehavend (top)	D-3	H11
Neisse River	F-3	H44
Nejd (right)	D-4	H35
Neuchâtel (top)	B-3	H31
Neustria	D-3	H 9
New Castilia (Peru) (left)		H29
New Granada (left)		H29
New Guinea (bottom)	D-4	H42
New Spain (left)		H29
Newfoundland	G-3	H45
Nicaea, Emp. of (bottom)	F-3	H13
Nicaragua (right)		H34
Nice (right)	B-3	H30
Nicomedia (left)	J-2	H13
Nimwegen (right)	A-2	H26
Nineveh (Ninus)	D-2	H 3
Nishapur (bottom)	H-3	H11
Nisibis (bottom)	F-2	H33
Nomonhan (bottom)	D-2	H40
Noricum	L-6	H 5
Normandy (top)	C-3	H42
Normandy, Duchy of	B-3	H18
Normans (top)	F-2	H13
North German Confederation (top)		H31
Northumbria	N-10	H10
Novara (right)	C-2	H30
Novgorod	D-1	H34
Novi (left)	D-5	H26
Numidia	K-7	H 5
Nürnberg (top)	D-3	H40
Nystad (top)	H-4	H34
Oder River	F-3	H44
Odessa (top)	G-3	H42
Offa's Dyke	C-2	H 9
Ohod, Mt. (top)	G-4	H11
Okinawa (bottom)	D-2	H42
Oldenburg (top)	C-2	H31
Oliva	A-3	H24
Olmütz (top)	E-3	H31
Olympus, Mt. (bottom)	C-1	H 4
Omayyad Empire (bottom)		H11
Omdurman (bottom)	E-4	H33
Oran (top)	D-4	H42
Orange, Princ. of	C-5	H20
Orange Free State (left)	E-9	H35
Orel (top)	G-2	H42
Ortuqids (bottom)	H-3	H13
Orléans	W-22	H17
Ostend	K-4	H37
Ostrogoths (East Goths)	J-3,F-3	H 7
Ostrolenka	A-4	H34
Ottoman Empire		H33
Oudenarde	G-3	H22
Outer Mongolia (right)	G-3	H35
Pacific Is., Terr. of the	T-5	H45
Pakistan	N-4	H45
Palatinate (top)	B-3	H31
Palestine (top)		H 4
Pallava Confederacy	Map C	H 2
Palmyra (Tadmor) (top)	E-2	H11
Palos	J-3	H19
Panamá		H29
Pannonia	L-6	H 5
Papal States (right)	E-3	H30
Paraguay (right)		H29
Paramushiru (bottom)	E-1	H42
Parma, Duchy of (right)	C-2	H30
Parnassus, Mt. (bottom)	C-2	H 4
Parthian Empire	O-7	H 5
Passarowitz	G-5	H23
Passchendaele	K-4	H37
Pavia	E-3	H 9
Pearl Harbor (bottom)	G-3	H42
Pechenegs (Patzinaks)	A-3	H34
Peipus, Lake	C-1	H34
Peking	F-2	H14
Peleliu (bottom)	D-3	H42
Pella (bottom)	C-1	H 4
Peloponnesus (bottom)	C-2	H 4
Pergamum	M-7	H 5
Pernambuco (Recife)		H29
Persepolis (bottom)	E-2	H 3
Persia (right)	D-4	H35
Persian Empire		H 5
Persis (bottom)	E-3	H 3
Peru (right)		H29
Petra (top)	D-4	H 4
Petsamo Dist.	H-2	H44
Philippines, Rep. of the	S-5	H45
Philippine Sea (bottom)	D-3	H42
Philistia (top)	D-4	H 4
Phoenicia (top)	D-2	H 4
Phrygian Kdm.	C-2	H 3
Piacenza (top)	D-2	H13
Pichincha (right)		H29
Picts	B-2	H 8
Piombino (bottom)	D-3	H30
Piraeus (bottom)	C-3	H 4
Pisa (left)	D-4	H15
Plassey	E-2	H14
Plataea (bottom)	C-2	H 4
Plevna (Pleven)	G-4	H36
Ploesti (top)	F-3	H42
Podolia	H-4	H21
Poitiers	O-16	H18
Poland, Kdm. of ("Congress Poland") (top)	F-2	H31
Poland, Partition of		H24
Polish Corridor (bottom)	D-2	H38
Pollentia	A-2	H 6
Polovtsi	D-2	H34
Poltava	J-5	H34
Pomerania	E-3	H14
Pompeii (bottom)	E-6	H 6
Pontus	N-6	H 5
Port Arthur	F-7	H34
Portugal	A-6	H21
Portugal, County of (top)	A-2	H13
Potsdam	F-3	H44
Prague	E-3	H21
Pressburg	J-4	H27
Preveza (top)	D-2	H33
Provence	E-4	H 9
Prussia, Kdm. of	C-2	H31
Prussians	F-3	H14
Przemyśl	G-3	H36
Pskov	H-2	H24
Puerto Rico		H29
Pydna (bottom)	C-1	H 4
Pyramids (top)	B-5	H 4
Qadisiya (top)	G-3	H11
Qain	J-3	H11
Quadi	L-6	H 5
Quebec	M-10	H22
Quemoy	R-4	H46
Quito		H29
Ragusa, Rep. of	F-5	H21
Rai	H-3	H11
Ramillies	H-3	H22
Rangoon (bottom)	B-3	H42
Raqqa (bottom)	F-3	H11
Rastatt	H-4	H22
Ravenna	E-4	H 7
Ravensberg (right)	D-1	H26
Red Russia	G-7	H24
Regensburg (Ratisbon)	H-4	H27
Reichstadt	F-3	H36
Réunion	M-7	H45
Reykjavík	B-2	H44
Rhaetia	K-6	H 5
Rhineland (top)	C-2	H40
Rhodes (bottom)	F-3	H13
Rhodesia (left)	E-8	H35
Riga	G-3	H38
Rio de Janeiro	G-7	H46
Rivoli (left)	E-4	H26
Rocoux (right)	A-3	H26
Romagna (right)	D-2	H30
Roman Empire		H 6
Rome (Roma)	D-4	H 6
Roncesvalles (bottom)	B-2	H11
Rossbach	E-3	H23
Roussillon	C-5	H21
Rubicon (Rubico)	D-2	H 6
Ruhr (top)	D-2	H42
Rum, Sult. of	H-3	H13
Rumania	G-4	H36
Russian Empire		H34
Ryswick	G-3	H22
Saar (top)	C-2	H40
Sabaean Kdm.	Map B	H 2
Sabines (Sabini)	D-3	H 6
Sadowa (top)	D-2	H31
St. Albans	C-3	H15
St. Mihiel	L-5	H37
St. Peter, Patrimony of (top)	E-2	H13
St. Petersburg	J-4	H34
St. Quentin	K-5	H37
Saipan (bottom)	E-3	H42
Sakaria River (bottom)	E-1	H33
Sakas	Map B	H 2
Sakhalin Island	G-6	H34
Saladin, Sultanate of (bottom)	G-4	H13
Salamis (bottom)	C-3	H 4
Salerno (top)	E-3	H42
Salian Franks	C-2	H 7
Saluzzo (left)	B-2	H30
Salzburg (left)	E-4	H26
Samaria (top)	D-3	H 4
Samarkand	D-2	H14
Samarra (bottom)	G-3	H11
Samo, Kdm. of	D-3	H 8
San Francisco	C-4	H46
San Marino	E-5	H20
San Salvador (Watling I.) (left)		H29
San Stefano	G-4	H36
Santa Fé Audiencia of (left)		H29
Santa Fé de Bogotá (left)		H29
Santa María del Buen Aire (left)		H29
Santiago		H29
Santo Domingo (left)		H29
São Sebastião do Rio de Janeiro (left)		H29
Saragossa	C-4	H15
Saragossa, Emirate of (top)	B-2	H13
Sarai	D-3	H34
Sarajevo	F-4	H36
Sardinia	J-5	H22
Sardinia, Kdm. of (right)	B-2,C-4	H30
Sardis (bottom)	B-2	H 3
Sarmatia	N-5	H 5
Sassanid Empire (top)	G-3	H13
Sasun (bottom)	F-2	H33
Savoy	H-4	H22
Saxa Rubra	B-4	H 6
Saxons	D-2	H 7
Saxony	J-2	H23
Scapa Flow	A-1	H37
Schleswig (top)	C-1	H31
Schmalkalden	E-3	H20
Scotland	B-2	H20
Scots	B-2	H 8
Scythians	Map B	H 2
Sedan (top)	B-3	H31
Seistan	J-3	H11
Seljuk Turks (top)	L-3	H13
Senussi (bottom)	D-3	H33
Serbia	E-4	H15
Serbia	G-4	H36
Sevastopol	A-5	H34
Seville	A-6	H20
Shanghai (bottom)	E-3	H40
Sheffield	C-2	H32
Shemakha	H-4	H15
Shimonoseki (right)	H-4	H35
Shirvan	H-3	H15
Siam (right)	G-5	H35
Sibir, Khanate of	K-2	H34
Sicily, Kdm. of	J-6	H22
Sidon (top)	D-3	H 4
Siena, Rep. of (left)	D-3	H30
Silesia	F-3	H23
Simla	N-4	H45
Sinai Pen. (top)	C-5	H 4
Singapore (bottom)	C-3	H42
Sinhala (Ceylon)	Map C	H 2
Sis (bottom inset)		H13
Sivas (top)	K-3	H13
Slavs	D-2,E-2,D-3	H 8
Slovakia (Prot.) (top)	D-3	H40
Smyrna (Izmir)	G-5	H38
Sogdiana	F-2	H 5
Soissons	J-1	H 9
Sokoto (left)	C-5	H35
Solferino (right)	D-2	H30
Solomon Is. (bottom)	E-4	H42
Solomon's Kdm. (top)	D-3	H 4
Somaliland	M-5	H45
Somme River	K-5	H37
Songhoy Empire	Map D	H 2
Sorbs	F-2	H 9
South Africa, Union of (left)	E-10	H35
South Manchuria R.R. (bottom)	E-4	H40
Southern Slovakia (top)	E-3	H40
Spain, Kdm. of	B-6	H21
Spanish Main (left)		H29
Spanish March	D-4	H 9
Spanish Nether-lands	C-3	H21
Sparta (bottom)	C-3	H 4
Srivijaya	F-3	H14
Stalingrad (top)	H-3	H42
Stilwell Road (bottom)	B-2	H42
Stockach (left)	D-4	H26
Stockholm	F-2	H23
Stralsund	E-3	H21
Strassburg	K-1	H 9
Strathclyde	N-10	H10
Stresa (top)	D-4	H38
Stuhlweissenburg	E-4	H15
Sudan	L-5	H45
Sudetenland (top)	D-2	H40
Suevi	E-2,A-4	H 7
Suevian Kingdom	B-3	H 8
Suez Canal	S-4	H41
Sumerian Civilization	Map A	H 2
Susa (bottom)	D-2	H 3
Sussex (Suthsaxona)	O-12	H10
Suzdal	D-2	H34
Swabia	D-4	H15
Swatow (bottom)	D-4	H40
Sweden, Kdm. of	G-1	H21
Swiss Confederation	D-4	H20
Syracuse (Syracusae)	E-6	H 6
Syria	L-4	H45
Syria (Aram) (top)	E-3	H 4
Tabaristan (bottom)	H-3	H11
Tagliacozzo	E-4	H15
Taif (top)	G-4	H11
Tanga (left)	F-7	H35
Tangier (top)	C-4	H42
Tangut Kdm.	F-1	H14
Tannu Tuva (bottom)	B-1	H42
Tarawa (bottom)	F-3	H42
Tarentum (Taranto)	F-4	H 6
Targowitz	N-11	H34
Tarsus (top)	D-1	H 4
Tartars (Tatars)	D-2	H34
Taxila	D-2	H14
Tehran	T-4	H41
Telamon	C-3	H 6
Tell el Amarna (top)	B-6	H 4
Tell el Kebir (bottom)	E-2	H33
Temesvar (top)	F-4	H31
Temple, le (bottom)	C-2	H42
Teplitz	H-3	H27
Teruel (top)	B-3	H40
Teschen (top)	E-3	H40
Teutonic Order, Dominion of the	G-2	H20
Thebes (No) (Egypt) (top)	D-5	H 3
Thebes (Greece) (bottom)	C-2	H 4
Thermopylae (bottom)	C-2	H 4
Thessalonica, Kingdom of	F-4	H15
Thessaly (bottom)	C-2	H 4
Thorn	K-10	H24
Thrace	M-6	H 5
Thule	F-2	H46
Thuringians	D-2	H 7
Ticinus	D-3	H 6
Tiflis (bottom)	K-2	H13
Tilsit	K-3	H27
Tlemcen	A-2	H33
Tmutarakan	A-3	H34
Togo (left)	C-6	H35
Tokugawa Shogunate	G-2	H14
Tokyo (bottom)	D-2	H42
Toledo	B-6	H20
Tolentino (left)	E-5	H26
Toulon (top)	D-3	H42
Toulouse	D-6	H18
Tournai	C-2	H 8
Tours (bottom)	C-2	H11
Trafalgar, Cape	A-6	H23
Trans-Siberian Railroad	D-6	H 34
Transvaal (left)	E-9	H35
Transylvania	G-4	H21
Trasimenus, Lake	D-3	H 6
Trebizond, Emp. of (bottom)	H-2	H13
Trieste	F-4	H44
Tripoli (left)	D-3	H35
Tripoli, County of (bottom inset)		H13
Trocadero	A-6	H28
Troy (Ilium) (bottom)	E-2	H 4
Troyes	X-21	H17
Truk (bottom)	E-3	H42
Tuileries, les (bottom)	B-2	H25
Tunis (left)	D-3	H35
Tunisia (left)	D-3	H35
Turin (right)	B-2	H30
Turkey (bottom)	E-2	H33
Tuscan Presidios	E-5	H21
Tuscany, Grand Duchy of (right)	D-3	H30
Tver	F-2	H34
Two Sicilies, Kdm. of (right)	F-5	H30
Tyre (top)	D-3	H 4
Ujiji (left)	F-7	H35
Ulithi (bottom)	D-3	H42
Ulm	E-4	H21
United Nations		H46
United Netherlands	C-3	H21
Upper Senegal & Niger (left)	B-5	H35
Uppsala (Upsala)	E-3	H15
Ur	C-2	H 3
Uruguay (right)		H29
Uryankhai (right)	F-3	H35
Ussuri District	G-6	H34
Utrecht	H-3	H22
Valais, Rep. of (left)	D-4	H26
Valmy (left)	C-4	H26
Valparaiso		H29
Van	F-2	H33
Vandals	F-2,C-5	H 7
Venaissin, County of (top)	D-3	H25
Vendée (left)	B-4	H26
Venezuela (right)		H29
Venice, Rep. of	E-4	H20
Vercellae	B-2	H 6
Verona	E-4	H15
Versailles	E-4	H38
Vesuvius, Mt.	E-4	H 6
Vichy (top)	D-3	H42
Vienna	F-4	H28
Vietnam	R-5	H46
Vilagos (top)	F-3	H31
Villafranca (right)	D-2	H30
Vilna	G-3	H38
Viminacium	G-4	H 7
Visigothic (West Gothic) Kdm.	B-3	H 8
Visigoths (West Goths)	H-3,C-4	H 7
Vitoria	E-5	H27
Vladimir	D-2	H34
Vladivostok	G-7	H34
Volga Bulgars, Kdm. of the	D-2	H34
Volhynia	C-2	H34
Volubilis (top)	B-3	H11
Voronez (top)	H-2	H42
Wadai (left)	D-5	H35
Wagram, Deutsch	J-4	H27
Wake I. (bottom)	F-3	H42
Wales	B-2	H12
Walili (bottom)	B-3	H11
Wallachia	D-1	H33
Walvis Bay (left)	D-9	H35
Warsaw (top)	F-3	H42
Warsaw, Duchy of	K-3	H27
Wasit (bottom)	G-3	H11
Waterloo	F-3	H27
Watling Street	D-3	H10
Wedmore	R-16	H10
Weihaiwei (right)	H-4	H35
Weimar (top)	F-3	H38
Wenden	H-2	H34
Wessex (West Saxonia)	O-12	H10
West Frankish Kdm.	M-2	H 9
West Gothic Kdm.	B-3	H 8
West Goths	H-3,C-4	H 7
West Prussia	F-7	H24
West Germany (Fed. Rep.)	E-3	H44
Western Roman Empire		H 7
Westphalia	G-3	H27
Whitby	S-14	H10
White Huns (Ephthalites)	D-2	H14
Wiltzes	F-2	H 9
Wittenberg	E-3	H20
Wittstock	E-3	H21
Woomera	S-7	H46
Worms	H-3	H16
Württemberg (top)	C-3	H31
Würzburg (left)	D-4	H26
Xerxes' Canal (bottom)	D-1	H 4
Yalta	L-3	H46
Yarmuk (top)	G-4	H11
Yavadvipa	Map C	H 2
Yedisan	E-1	H33
Yemama (bottom)	G-4	H11
Yenan (bottom)	R-4	H46
York	S-15	H10
Ypres	K-4	H37
Yugoslavia	F-4	H38
Zab (bottom)	G-3	H11
Zangids (bottom)	J-3	H13
Zara	F-4	H36
Zeebrugge	K-4	H37
Zeirids (bottom)	E-3	H13
Zenta (bottom)	C-1	H33
Ziyanids (top)	A-4	H13
Zululand (left)	F-9	H35
Zürich (left)	D-4	H26

Mary Jaffe